ISBN: 979-8-9916101-3-1

Warriors For His Glory is a 501c3 non-profit organization.

www.WarriorsForHisGlory.com

This book is dedicated to three people who stood their ground when the fight was heavy.

To my wife, Holly

You are the backbone of our family and the steady presence behind every step I take. You have carried more than your share, loved without condition, and stood firm when the cost was high. Your strength, patience, and faith have anchored me when I wavered. You are the love of my life, and none of this would exist without you.

To my brother and friend, Christian Williams

You have walked beside me with honesty and conviction, never letting me settle for shallow faith or comfortable excuses. You push me forward when I stall, call me higher when I drift, and remind me who I am when I forget. Your friendship has sharpened my walk with God more than you know.

To my brother and friend, Kurt Bush

You poured yourself into this book with tireless commitment while simultaneously walking into the pain of hundreds of veterans, helping them confront wounds most people never see. Your heart for healing, your persistence, and your willingness to shoulder the weight alongside me helped bring this work to life. This book bears your fingerprints.

This work exists because of love, brotherhood, and faith lived out in the trenches.

Thank you for standing with me.

INTRODUCTION

The night was quiet. Too quiet in fact. Then came the blast.

It wasn't just the explosion that rattled the air, it was the aftermath. Silence. Dust. Screams muffled by ringing ears. A heartbeat pounding so hard you swear the whole world can hear it. This is where the battle begins. Not on some faraway battlefield, but in the mind.

For some, PTSD doesn't announce itself with banners or warnings. It creeps in like a fog, unseen until you're already lost in it. One moment you're laughing with friends, and the next, you're drowning in memories that feel more real than the present. One wrong sound, one passing smell, one flash of light and suddenly you're right back there in the middle of it. The walls close in. The heart races. The fight-or-flight instincts surge, but there's nowhere to run.

This is the invisible war, and friend, you are not alone in it.

In war, the enemy is normally clear. You can see their weapons, map their movements, and plan your counterattack. But PTSD? It doesn't wear a uniform. It doesn't announce its advance. It ambushes you when you least expect it, in the grocery store aisle, at the family dinner table, or in the dead of night when you should be at peace. It's the war no one sees but you and if you've been in that fight, you know how brutal it can be.

The sleepless nights. The weight of guilt and shame. The flashbacks that don't ask permission. The feeling that maybe, just maybe, you're broken beyond repair.

But here's the truth no one ever told you: you are not broken. You are a warrior under fire.

This book is not a soft pillow and a blanket; it's a battle plan. It's not here to coddle you, it's here to equip you. We're going to talk about faith. We're going to talk about scars. We're going to talk about what it means to walk through the valley and keep moving when your legs want to quit.

Jesus never promised us an easy fight, but He did promise us victory. He said, *"In this world you will have trouble. But take heart! I have overcome the world"* (John 16:33). You may feel outnumbered. You may feel ambushed. But you are not out of options. You have weapons. You have brothers. You have a God who has not abandoned you.

This isn't about pretending the war isn't real, rather it's about facing it head-on. You've carried wounds. You've faced losses. You've walked through fire. And yet here you are, reading these words, still standing. That means one thing: you are still in the fight!

In these pages, you'll find strategies for the battlefield of the mind, stories of warriors who refused to quit, and reminders from God's Word that you are never fighting alone. We will take ground, inch by inch if we have to, and we will not retreat.

Because PTSD does not get the final word...Not today...Not tomorrow...Not ever!

Before you turn the page, take a breath and remember this: You are not defined by what happened to you, you are defined by the One who walks with you through it.

The fight isn't over, friend, it's just beginning.

Welcome to the war.

Now, let's get faith fueled and battle-ready.

Chapter 1: Welcome to the Fight: Naming the Enemy, Following Our General

I once sat with a Marine who looked like he could crush a steel beam with his bare hands. But when we started talking, I noticed his jaw clench every time the conversation drifted anywhere near "what's going on inside." His eyes flicked back and forth like he was scanning a battlefield only he could see.

Finally, he leaned back and said, "You know what's messed up? The war followed me home. It crawled inside my head, and now no matter what I do, I'm fighting a battle I can't win."

That was his verdict: unwinnable.

This may or may not be the same feelings you are dealing with, but that's how post-traumatic stress disorder is often described, like you're still carrying the weight of the battlefield inside you with no way to shut it off. Sleepless nights. Fists through drywall. Snapping at family for no reason. Hypervigilance in every crowded space. And when it piles up, it whispers the deadliest lie: "This is who you are now."

And maybe, in your own way, you've felt the same. It might not look exactly like his fight, but the battlefield in your mind feels just as real. That's how many describe living with post-traumatic stress disorder, like you're carrying the weight of the battlefield inside you and there's no way to shut it off.

Sleepless nights. Fists through drywall. Snapping at your kids or spouse for no reason. Hypervigilance in every crowded space. And when it all piles up, it whispers the deadliest lie: "This is who you are now."

But hear me clearly: that's not the truth.

PTSD is real, but it is not your identity. It's an injury, just as real as shrapnel wounds or broken bones. Nobody calls a man weak when

5

he takes shrapnel; they call him wounded. Yet when the wound is invisible, buried in the mind and soul, the world slaps labels like "unstable," "crazy," or "broken" on him. And if you're not careful, you start to believe those labels yourself.

That Marine? He wasn't crazy. He wasn't beyond repair. He was wounded, like so many others who've faced unspeakable battles, in combat, on the streets, or even at home. He needed to hear what I'm telling you now, "You're not fighting this battle alone and the fight is not unwinnable!"

Jesus said in John 10:10, *"The thief comes only to steal and kill and destroy; I have come that they may have life, and have it to the full."*

The thief is real and there is no doubt about that. He's the voice that whispers shame, the one that tells you that you'll never be free, the one that keeps you locked in guilt and fear. That's the enemy. Not your wife. Not your buddies. Not even your own mind. The true enemy is the liar who wants you to believe the darkness is permanent. But Jesus didn't stop at exposing the thief's plan. He declared the opposite, "I have come so that you might have life — and have it to the full."

If John 10:10 was only the first half of the verse there wouldn't be much comfort in it, but we can't miss the second half of that verse as that is what changes everything. Jesus says He came so that you might have life, real life, not just survival mode. And He came not as a distant figure but as the General who leads from the front. He knows the battlefield of the mind. He knows the cost of war. And He doesn't leave His soldiers behind.

David understood this better than most which he demonstrated in writing Psalm 139:11-12, *"If I say, 'Surely the darkness will hide me and the light become night around me,' even the darkness will not be dark to you; the night will shine like the day, for darkness is as light to you."*

The Hebrew word for darkness that is used in the original writing is choshek and its definition isn't just the absence of light like we would think of in English. Rather, it is referring to oppressive, suffocating, heavy. And yet David says even in that place, God sees perfectly. In other words, your General has eyes on you, even in the blackout...even in the pain...even in the suffocation...even in the oppressive darkness.

And Paul reinforces it in 2 Corinthians 1:3–4 when he says: *"Praise be to the God and Father of our Lord Jesus Christ, the Father of compassion and the God of all comfort, who comforts us in all our troubles."* When he says comforts us in all our troubles, Paul wasn't talking about theory. Consider this, Paul been shipwrecked three times, beaten with rods, stoned and left for dead, chained in prison cells, betrayed, and ultimately executed - and yet he still declared God as the God of comfort.

That's the enemy named and the General known. PTSD isn't who you are. The thief doesn't get the last word. And the General doesn't just bark orders, He steps into the foxhole with you and says, "Follow me. We're going through this together."

As we step forward into the pages ahead, I want you to know this: God is not some distant general barking out orders while hiding behind a desk from miles away. He is right there in the midst of the battle with you. He's the One who crawls into the mud beside you, who feels the weight of your battles, and who refuses to abandon you when the fire is hottest. Scripture reminds us, *"The LORD is near to the brokenhearted and saves the crushed in spirit"* (Psalm 34:18). That means right now, yes, even in the middle of your struggles, God is closer than the air you breathe.

You are not just a soldier left to fight alone, you are a beloved son of the King. God loves you more than you can imagine or comprehend, and His love is not conditional on your performance, your strength, or your track record. He cares for you in ways the world never could and He wants you to be whole. He wants you to feel His arms wrapping around you, steadying you when you stumble, and lifting you when you fall. Jesus said plainly, *"As the Father has loved me, so have I loved you. Now remain in my love"* (John 15:9). That's not theory, that's reality.

But this journey isn't only about encouragement; it's also about equipping. In the chapters to come, we'll dive into practical approaches that can help you move forward in the healing process. You'll learn how to fight through compromise, how to armor yourself against temptation, how to stand firm when life gets overwhelming, and how to embrace the brotherhood God has placed around you. These aren't abstract ideas. They're battle-tested truths you can grab onto, live out, and see make a difference in your daily fight.

So as we continue, I want you to lean in with expectation. Open your heart to the reality that God is here, that He loves you fiercely, and that He has already prepared the tools you'll need to overcome. This isn't just a book, it's a field manual for your soul and together, we are going to march through it one chapter at a time, side by side with the Commander who has already guaranteed the victory.

Drills & Practice

When the military trains soldiers, drills aren't optional. They're repeated until they become instinct. We couldn't wait until rounds were flying overhead to wonder how to clear a room, it would have already been too late. Instead, we trained until it was muscle memory.

Spiritual and mental resilience work the same way. These drills may feel simple, even repetitive, but that's the point. They rewire your brain, re-anchor your spirit, and create reflexes for when the fight shows up uninvited.

Box Breathing 4×4×4×4

- How: Inhale for four seconds. Hold for four. Exhale for four. Hold for four. Repeat until your heart rate slows.
- Why it matters: This isn't fluff, it's science. Special operations units use this because it calms the nervous system under extreme stress. Trauma keeps your body stuck on red alert but this drill flips the switch back down.
- Faith Connection: Genesis tells us God breathed life into

man. With every inhale, you're receiving His breath. With every exhale, you're handing fear back to Him.

Grounding 5-4-3-2-1

- How: Name 5 things you see, 4 things you feel, 3 things you hear, 2 things you smell, 1 thing you taste.
- Why it matters: Flashbacks try to drag you back into the past. Grounding reminds your brain you're in the present. Counselors use this worldwide because it works.
- Faith Connection: Psalm 46:10 says, "Be still, and know that I am God." Grounding forces you to pause, notice, and recognize God's presence where you actually are.

Breath Prayer

- How: With each inhale: "When I am afraid..." With each exhale: "...I trust in You." (Psalm 56:3).
- Why it matters: Short prayers linked to breathing calm both body and spirit. Studies show repeating truth rewires stress pathways.
- Faith Connection: This isn't self-help, It's God-help. You're using your breath to echo back God's Word, letting His truth override fear.
- Practice these daily. Not just when panic strikes. The more you train, the faster your body and spirit respond when the ambush comes.

Thought & Discussion Questions

- What battles are you fighting right now that feel unwinnable?
- Which lies of the thief have you believed about yourself?

- Where have you seen God's presence in the dark places of your life?
- Which of these drills will you commit to practicing daily this week?

After Action Report & Mission Orders

In the military, an After Action Review (AAR) is where we process the mission such as what worked, what didn't, and what's next. These Mission Orders aren't "homework." They're steps toward reclaiming your ground.

Your first mission isn't about winning the war all at once. It's about small victories, one day at a time.

- Read Psalm 139 daily. Circle every word about God's presence. Let it remind you the General sees you even in the dark.
- Check in with a buddy three times this week. Brotherhood is oxygen. Don't isolate, go ahead and send a text, grab coffee, or make the call.
- Start your SITREP journal. Each day record:
    - Situation (what happened)
    - Feelings (be real)
    - God's Truth (Scripture that speaks into it)
    - Next Step (what you'll do)

By week's end, you will begin to see God's fingerprints in the middle of your struggle.

Chapter 2: From Labels to Legacy: Identity in Christ

I once sat with a soldier who told me he hated mirrors. Not because of scars or disfigurement that he had from battle, but because of the names he saw written all over himself whenever he looked at his own reflection.

To him, his reflection just showed...Failure...Monster...Anger problem...Unfit father...Drunk.

There was no need for some enemy to be there throwing those labels and names at him, he had his own mind replaying the labels for himself on an endless loop. Every bad decision, every regret, every night that ended with a fist through drywall or a wife crying on the couch, piled into a verdict: this is who you are. Even though he'd served honorably, had performed with valor in battle, and carried the scars of combat, the only identity he recognized and claimed for himself was failure.

And here's the cruel thing about trauma, it doesn't just mess with your memories, it messes with your identity. PTSD doesn't just leave you with sleepless nights; it tattoos your soul with labels you never asked for. That's what labels do, they get tattooed on the soul, and you start to believe that they are permanent and true. PTSD piles more on...unstable...broken...damaged goods...and then it's just slow death by a thousand name-tags.

Every false label is a weapon the enemy tries to use to wound you, but we mustn't forget those labels are not forged in heaven, and they carry no eternal authority. God alone speaks the final verdict over your life, and His decree is victory, redemption, and sonship through Christ. *"See what great love the Father has lavished on us, that we should be called children of God! And that is what we are"* (1 John 3:1). That truth, not the accusations of people or the enemy, gets the last word.

Paul writes in 2 Corinthians 5:17, *"Therefore, if anyone is in Christ, the new creation has come: The old has gone, the new is here!"* The Greek word Paul used in the original text for "new" there is kainos and it's fascinating because it doesn't mean "slightly upgraded" or "patched up." It means brand new, fresh out of the box. He is explaining to us that the old isn't duct-taped together; it's just gone and completely replaced. In Christ, you're not just a repaired version of your old self, you are a brand-new creation.

And in Ephesians 2:10, Paul drives it home with, *"For we are God's workmanship, created in Christ Jesus to do good works, which God prepared in advance for us to do."* Paul is saying that you are not a mistake or an afterthought, but rather you are something intentionally crafted, shaped, designed. A masterpiece! You're not junk and you're not a mistake. You're a crafted work that is God's own poem, written into existence with purpose.

Paul continues in Romans 8:15 when he says, *"The Spirit you received brought about your adoption to sonship. And by him we cry, 'Abba, Father.'"* This is one of my favorite examples of understanding the original language changing or enhancing scripture I previously thought I understood.

The word Paul uses for adoption is huiothesia and it is a legal term used at that time that meant full status, full rights, full inheritance, full status as a son. You aren't an afterthought and you don't get in the back door of God's family as a charity case, you get the full seat at the table, name and all.

You see what's happening here? The General is handing you a new set of orders. He's tearing off the old nametags and pinning on your true identity.

Now that Marine I mentioned earlier, Matt, he wrestled with labels like "broken" and "dangerous." He wrestled with these labels for weeks and every time we'd meet, he'd circle back to the same question: "Yeah, I hear you, but what if I screw up again?" My answer was simple: You probably will...and so will I. Heck, look at scripture, Peter did. So did David. So did Paul. But screwing up doesn't make you a screw-up, it makes you human.

The difference in moving forward or staying in the never-ending pain loop is determined by whether you stay chained to the old labels or start walking in the new legacy Christ has written for you. Think about it, the same Peter who denied Jesus three times was the same man Jesus later put in charge of feeding His sheep. Paul, who once hunted Christians, became the author of half the New Testament. God specializes in taking men with a bad rap sheet and turning them into men with a bold legacy.

One night in our recovery group Matt finally said, "I don't want my kids to grow up thinking Dad was just an angry drunk who couldn't keep it together." That was the turning point for Matt. Because that's what labels do, they will freeze you in a moment. But thankfully God doesn't deal in labels, He deals in legacy. Legacy is what you hand down when the fight is over. It's the story your kids tell about you, it's the testimony your brothers in Christ share about your life. And if you're in Christ, your legacy isn't "failure," it's "faithful." It's not "drunk," it's "disciple." It's not "abandoned," it's "adopted."

This isn't just scented candles, meditation, or positive thinking, it's blood-bought reality. Jesus didn't go to the cross so you could limp through life with a stack of shame taped to your chest. He died and rose again to give you a new name, a new purpose, and a new mission.

Drills & Practice

Identity isn't rebuilt by accident. Just like a soldier retrains muscle memory after an injury, you've got to retrain your mind to embrace the truth of who you are in Christ. These drills are about rewiring your thoughts, breaking down lies, and reinforcing God's truth until it becomes second nature.

1. Truth Replacement Card

- How: Write down three lies you keep hearing in your head. Next to each, write a verse that speaks God's truth against it. Check out this example: Lie - "I'm a failure." Truth - *"I can do all things through Christ who strengthens me"* (Philippians 4:13).
- Why: Psychology calls it "cognitive restructuring." The Bible calls it *"taking every thought captive"* (2 Corinthians 10:5). Either way, your brain can learn to reject lies when truth is rehearsed often enough.
- Faith Connection: Jesus Himself used Scripture to shut down Satan in the wilderness (Matthew 4). If it worked for Him, it will work for you.

2. Identity Creed
- How: Write out a personal declaration of who you are in Christ, anchored in Scripture. Read it aloud every morning and every night.
- Why: Speaking truth reinforces it. Studies show vocal repetition builds stronger neural pathways than silent thought.
- Faith Connection: Romans 10:17 says, *"Faith comes from hearing, and hearing through the word of Christ."* Hearing yourself proclaim truth builds faith.

3. Lectio Divina on Ephesians 2:10
- How: Read the verse four times. First, just read it. Second, reflect on a word or phrase that stands out. Third, respond with a short prayer. Fourth, rest and listen.
- Why: Trauma wires you to stay on high alert. This practice forces you to slow down and engage

Scripture deeply.

- ○ **Faith Connection: God's Word isn't just information, it's transformation. This method lets Scripture get from your head into your heart.**

Thought & Discussion Questions

1. Which labels have stuck to you the hardest, and how have they shaped how you see yourself?
2. When you hear that you are a "new creation" in Christ, what stirs in you? Hope, doubt, resistance, relief?
3. If you were to write a line in your Identity Creed today, what would it say?
4. How does the truth of being adopted into God's family challenge the lies you've believed about yourself?

After Action Report & Mission Orders

Your mission this week is to start tearing off old labels and replacing them with truth.

1. Recite your Identity Creed morning and night. Keep it simple but scriptural. Let it set the tone for your day and the anchor for your night.
2. Create your Truth Replacement Card. Carry it in your pocket or phone. When lies show up, hit back with truth.
3. Memorize 2 Corinthians 5:17. Drill it until it's automatic. This is your rally cry verse for the week.
4. Check in with your buddy. Share your Identity Creed with him. Pray for each other to believe the truth you're declaring.

Chapter 3: Battlefield of the Mind – Renew, Reframe, Replace

I worked with a soldier named Derrick who told me the war moved into his head. He said it without drama and more in a tone that was just tired honesty that felt heavier than body armor. A smell from the grill, a car backfiring down the street, a news clip with sand and sirens, and his pulse would spike like he was back outside the wire. His hands would tighten and clench and his jaw locked. He ultimately knew in his mind he was standing on green grass in his backyard, but his body does not care.

When he explained how he had learned to overcome this, I was fascinated. Here is what Derrick learned to say out loud, and what you and I must learn to admit. Because the hardest fights don't start with fists or bullets, they start with thoughts. A single thought slips in, feelings rush to meet it, and actions fall in line. You think, then you feel, then you do. That is the chain of command inside your life.

You know this chain by heart.

> You think: I am trapped.
> You feel: fear and anger.
> You act: you shut down or you blow up.

> Or you think: I am a failure.
> You feel: shame and heaviness.
> You act: you isolate or reach for a bottle.

Trauma knows how to pull this chain and PTSD trains the threat center of your brain to hit the alarm even when there is no enemy at the door. Don't misunderstand, you are not weak for feeling it, you are wired for it after what you have seen and survived. Good news follows that hard truth though. God made our minds with the ability to be renewed, so what has been wired by trauma can be rewired by truth.

Most of us let thoughts fly overhead like incoming rounds and only react once they detonate. Scripture will not let us live that way though as the General has given us orders for this fight.

Paul says, do not conform to the pattern of this world, but be transformed by the renewing of your mind. That word for transformed in Romans 12 verse 2 is not a coat of paint to just cover up the issue, it is a full renovation. Rip the old studs out and put the new structure in. God does not ask you to slap a smile over a storm, He steps into the house and rebuilds it from the foundation through the frame.

The question I have asked hundreds of times is, why do we struggle so much to follow these orders? The answer is simple and honest...trauma edits our brains. In our brains we have a small item called the amygdala. Even though it is small it plays a massive role in how we process emotions and respond to the world around us as it helps generate and regulate emotions like fear, anger, and pleasure. It works with the hippocampus to attach emotions to memories which is why our emotionally charged events are often easier to remember.

The amygdala works as our alarm system but through our traumatic experiences it has learned to call wolves where there are only wind and shadows. It basically floods our body with stress as if the past is happening right now in the present. We can tell ourselves to relax but somehow our foot still stays on the gas. This is why a simple command to quit thinking about it never works, you cannot simply white knuckle a broken circuit back into place.

Our God is a loving father and our creator, so he understands what is going on and does not ask us to ignore our thoughts. Instead, he tells us to renew them, to reframe them, and to replace them. That is the process, but what does it really mean?

Renew means new thinking built by new truth. You let the Word of God move from the page into your patterns. You read, you reflect, you practice, you repeat. Over time the Spirit rewires our brains pathways and science calls this neuroplasticity but long before science, research studies, and psychologists, the Bible told you first that your mind can be made new.

Reframe means you put on the correct lens. Philippians 4:8 says, "Finally, brothers and sisters, whatever is true, whatever is noble, whatever is right, whatever is pure, whatever is lovely, whatever is admirable—if anything is excellent or praiseworthy—think about such things." Paul did not write this as some poetry for a kitchen poster; it is a filter for every thought. Whatever is true, whatever is noble, whatever is right, whatever is pure, whatever is lovely, whatever is admirable. Hold the thought up to that light. If it fails the test, it does not get to march in your head. You do not drink from a muddy canteen when clear water is in reach.

Replace is where courage shows up. Second Corinthians 10:5 says, "We demolish arguments and every pretension that sets itself up against the knowledge of God, and we take captive every thought to make it obedient to Christ." Focus on Paul's statement that we take every thought captive and make it obey Christ, that is not a suggestion. It is an order. You don't argue with a hostile thought, instead you arrest it, strip it of weapons, and bring it before the General. Then you speak a better word.

The thought says: I cannot handle this.

Truth answers: I can do all things through Christ who strengthens me.

The thought says: I am worthless.

Truth answers: I am fearfully and wonderfully made.

Do this once and it feels clumsy. Do it again and, well, unfortunately, it feels awkward. Four or five times in, well, it might still feel awkward. Do it daily though and you will begin to wear new trails through your mind. Thoughts become beliefs and beliefs shape identity. Identity is important as it sets your direction. You must remain vigilant though because if you refuse to capture your thoughts, they will capture you.

The battlefield of the mind will never remain neutral, either you take dominion through Christ, or those thoughts will chain you in captivity. But when you drag them into the light of Jesus, something powerful shifts. Under His authority, your thoughts begin to lose their power to rule you. Instead of being a slave to your mind, you become a warrior steward of it. The lies start bowing. The temptations lose their grip. The storm in your head finds its Commander. And as you submit them to Christ, you will discover that, little by little, they start submitting to you.

This is why the chain matters. Think with truth, feel with clarity, act with courage. Our General is not shouting from the rear, He is at the front, steady and sure, calling you to follow. Win this fight in the head and your feet will follow.

Drills and Practice

Training is not punishment, it is preparation. Training is freedom when the fight comes, because it builds muscle memory for the soul so we are able to instinctually act. These drills aren't busywork; they are weapons forged in the quiet before the war breaks out. Each exercise helps you track the chain reaction, from thought to feeling to action, and then snap it with the truth of God's Word before it drags you into defeat. Work them every day. Grind them into your spirit. So that when the ambush comes, and it will definitely come, you won't freeze or fumble. You'll move with the instinct of a trained warrior. Ready. Steady. Dangerous to the enemy.

1. Thought Record
   ○ **Sit down with paper or your journal and name the situation. Write the first thought that hit you. Name the feeling that followed and rate its intensity. Describe what you did next.**

- Now add God's truth that speaks to that thought, and write one next step that lines up with that truth.
- You are drawing a map through your mind so you can pick a better route next time. Over days and weeks you will see patterns, and patterns are places where change can start.

2. Philippians 4:8 Meditation
   - Pick one phrase from the verse, for example whatever is true. Sit still for five minutes. Breathe slow. Repeat that phrase while you breathe. Let other thoughts pass by without a fight. Bring your attention back to the phrase. You are not emptying your mind. You are filling it with the command of God. Peace follows practice. Focus builds strength.

3. Reframing
   - Take one recurring thought that drags you down. Write it on a blank page. Under it, make two columns.
   - In one, evidence for and in the other, evidence against. Be honest. When both columns are full, write one clear sentence of Scripture truth that corrects the lie.
   - Read that sentence out loud. Put it on a card. Keep it close. You are not pretending the past did not happen. You are refusing to let a distorted story call the plays.

These drills will not erase your scars and that's a good thing; scars are proof you've been in the fight. They're reminders that you took the hit, but you're still standing. Every scar carries a story: some of shame, some of survival, and some of God's mercy written across your flesh and your soul. I've got scars myself, and when I trace them, whether it's those on my body or in my memory, they remind me that God was there in the foxhole with me. They remind me that pain doesn't get the last word, because healing leaves its mark too.

What these drills will do is give you skill. They'll hardwire reflex into your bones. They'll teach you to meet fear with truth and panic with God's presence. Just like soldiers train until every movement is second nature, these practices can become your second nature too. You don't wait until the bullets fly to learn how to fight, you drill until you can't get it wrong.

The psalmist declared in Psalm 144:1, "Blessed be the Lord, my rock, who trains my hands for war, and my fingers for battle." That's not just about swinging a sword in some ancient battlefield, that's about today and that is about us. It's about God Himself stepping in as your trainer, sharpening your instincts, teaching you how to fight in His strength.

So don't despise your scars. Wear them as proof that you've been tested and lived to tell about it. But don't stop there. Train. Drill. Prepare. Because the next battle is coming, and when it does, you won't be scrambling for your weapon, you'll already have it in hand.

Thought & Discussion Questions

1. Which thought patterns ambush you most often, and what do they push you to do?
2. How would your actions change if your first response was to test a thought against Philippians 4:8?
3. What is one lie that needs to be arrested, and what single verse will you use to replace it?
4. Where do you sense our General inviting you to practice renewal this week?

After Action Report & Mission Orders

Your orders for this week are simple and clear. Execute them with focus.

1. Complete three Thought Records. Do not wait for perfect timing. As soon as a trigger hits, write it down, trace it, and answer it with truth.
2. Memorize Philippians 4:8. Recite it in the morning and at night. Use it as the filter for the day.
3. Practice five minutes of Scripture meditation daily. Choose one phrase from Philippians 4:8 and stay with it.
4. Buddy check in. Share one reframed truth with your brother. Pray for each other to hold the line when the ambush comes.

Chapter 4: The War of Lies - Recognizing Triggers and Countering Deception

Stepping deeper into the battlefield doesn't always come with the roar of gunfire or the blast of bombs. Sometimes the most dangerous ground looks calm, silent even. Think about a soldier walking through a minefield. There's no shouting enemy, no bullets flying, no visible threat. But as we all know, every step is a risk. One wrong move and the explosion comes without warning.

That's what spiritual warfare feels like more often than not. It's not always the big, loud attacks that take men out. Sometimes it's the subtle traps: a slow compromise, a lingering temptation, a thought you let run unchecked. The enemy doesn't always charge at you head-on; sometimes he waits, patient and quiet, like a sniper hidden in the brush or a landmine buried just beneath the surface.

I've seen men crumble not because of a major blow but because of little things that slipped in unnoticed. The grudge they held onto. The private sin they justified. The bitterness they never dug out. No grenades went off in their life, just a slow erosion of strength until they couldn't stand anymore.

This is why vigilance matters. This is why our training matters. We're not just bracing for the obvious battles; we're preparing for the hidden ones too. Paul reminded us in 2 Corinthians 2:11 that we must not be ignorant of Satan's schemes, "so that we would not be outwitted by Satan; for we are not ignorant of his designs." The minefield is real. The enemy's traps are real. But so is God's power to guide our steps if we're listening, if we're disciplined, if we're battle-ready.

I remember working with a Marine named Jake. He was as squared away as they come; strong, sharp, disciplined. But he carried a lie deep in his heart: "I failed my brothers, and God could never forgive me." That thought was a landmine he stepped on every day. It triggered guilt that ate him alive and that guilt fueled the isolation that made him push away his family, his church, and every ounce of hope.

The enemy never had to storm Jake's defenses or launch an obvious attack. He didn't need bombs or bullets, just a single lie planted deep in Jake's heart. That lie became a leash and every time Jake tried to step forward, it yanked him back. Every time he tried to lift his head, the weight of guilt pulled it down.

That's how the devil works, he doesn't always fight like an army charging the gates. Sometimes he fights like a parasite, sinking one thought into your soul and feeding on it until you're hollow. He knows that if he can keep your eyes locked on shame, you'll never look up to see grace. If he can keep your ears tuned to the whisper of failure, you'll never hear the roar of God's forgiveness. He doesn't need to overpower you; he just needs to keep you focused on the wrong thing long enough to destroy you from the inside out.

That's why Scripture tells us in John 8:44 that the devil 'is a liar and the father of lies.' Lies are his primary weapon. He doesn't have to take Jake, or you, head-on when he can keep you circling the same battlefield in your own mind, convinced you've already lost. The lie becomes the battlefield, and if you don't drag it into the light of God's truth, it will bury you just as surely as any ambush. And isn't that exactly what happens to us far too often?

During World War II, the Nazis launched a deception mission called Operation Greif in the thick of the Battle of the Bulge. Instead of charging with tanks or overwhelming the front lines, they sent German soldiers disguised in stolen American uniforms. These infiltrators didn't march with heavy guns; they carried confusion as their weapon. They flipped road signs to send convoys the wrong way. They delivered false orders to reroute entire units. They whispered doubt and mistrust into the ranks like poison in the water supply.

The results were devastating. Allied soldiers began to question everyone and everything. Men arrested their own brothers-in-arms, unsure if they were genuine or disguised. Panic spread faster than artillery fire. Friend looked at friend and wondered if he was the enemy in disguise.

And here's the sobering truth: the enemy didn't need to overpower the American forces with bullets. They just needed to plant doubt. They weren't winning through sheer strength; they weakened their opponents by turning trust into suspicion and unity into division.

That's exactly how the devil works in our lives, he doesn't always charge head-on. Sometimes he comes in disguise, slipping lies into your thinking, flipping the signs on your moral compass, rerouting your confidence in God, and making you question the people who should be your allies. He knows that if he can get you to second-guess God's Word, or doubt the brotherhood He placed around you, he doesn't need to fire a shot. The battle is already halfway lost.

That's why Proverbs 3:5-6 warns us to "Trust in the Lord with all your heart and lean not on your own understanding." Without trust in God's voice and clarity from His truth, we are vulnerable to infiltration. And that's why we're called to "test the spirits" in 1 John 4:1 and to "be alert and of sober mind" in 1 Peter 5:8. The enemy loves to wear our uniform but when we know the Commander's voice and march by His orders, no imposter can lead us astray.

Satan does this to us every single day. He slips into our heads disguised as a thought that sounds like our own voice: "You're worthless. You're broken. You're dangerous. You'll never change." And just like those infiltrators, the lie doesn't look foreign. It looks like it belongs.

If you don't test it against the General's battle orders, that lie will turn you against yourself, against your brothers, even against God. This is why Jesus called the devil the "father of lies" in John 8:44. It's his native language and the best way to fight a liar is to drag his words into the light.

When Satan tempted Jesus in the wilderness, he twisted scripture. He tried to infiltrate Jesus' mind with lies disguised as truth. But every time, Jesus answered with the written Word. Not with his feelings and emotions. Not with debate or apologetics. He answered with the General's orders.

That's the same weapon we carry. The Word of God unmasks the lie and once you expose it, the confusion fades, and you can see clearly again.

For Jake, the trigger was a memory of the firefight where his buddy didn't make it home. For someone else, it might be the smell of diesel, the sound of fireworks, or even just a quiet room that feels too empty. Triggers are those tripwires the enemy uses to set off explosions in your heart and mind. When you know what they are, you can disarm them, but when you don't, you're walking through a minefield blindfolded.

Naming the lie attached to the trigger is the first step in taking its power away.

Drills & Practice

1. Write down the lies you've been carrying. If it feels risky to admit, that's the point.
2. Counter each lie with Scripture. Not vague positivity but instead concrete, battle-ready truth.
3. Practice speaking truth out loud. When you hear your own voice declare God's orders, it reinforces the truth in your spirit.

Looking for evidence that these drills actually work? Psychologists and neuroscientists are finally catching up to what the Bible has said for thousands of years. Repeated thoughts rewire your brain. Romans 12:2 wasn't exaggerating when it told us to be transformed by the renewing of our minds. When you replace lies with God's truth consistently, your brain literally reshapes itself.

Thought & Discussion Questions

1. What lies have you found circling in your head the longest?
2. How have those lies shaped your feelings or actions?
3. Can you identify a specific "trigger" in your life and the lie tied to it?
4. Which Scripture verse has the most power in exposing that lie?
5. How does the story of Operation Greif change the way you view the enemy's tactics today?

After Action Report & Mission Orders

1. Take stock of your week. Did you identify a lie? How did you counter it? Did it make a difference in how you felt or acted?
2. Mission Orders: Choose one lie you're going to drag into the light this week. Write it down. Find one Scripture that cuts it down. Every time the lie surfaces, speak that verse out loud. Make it your weapon until it becomes automatic.

Remember: you're not just surviving the ambush; you're learning to fight back.

Chapter 5: The Ambush of Shame – Breaking Free from the Past

Every soldier knows the ambush is the deadliest attack. You're not ready for it. You're walking, maybe even joking with the guy next to you, and suddenly the world explodes. That's what shame does, it doesn't just come from your past, it waits in the shadows for the right moment to strike.

Shame is different from guilt. Guilt says, "I did something wrong." Shame says, "I am something wrong." And when shame sets the ambush, it doesn't just hit your emotions, it rewires your identity.

I once worked with a soldier named David who had seen combat, but his real war was inside. He kept replaying a moment when he felt he had frozen under fire, convinced that if he'd moved faster, a buddy would still be alive. Every night, the ambush came again, the same moment, the same condemnation: "You're a coward. You're a failure. You're unworthy of forgiveness."

That was David's battle and here's what shame still does, it builds a prison without bars. You can laugh, work, even go to church, but inside, you're still sitting in solitary confinement, replaying the worst day of your life.

Why does the enemy love shame so much? Because it feels final. Guilt can be dealt with through confession and repentance. But shame whispers, "This is who you are. You'll never change."

That isn't from God. The General never defines His soldiers by their failures. Look at the Apostle Peter, I mean he denied Christ three times immediately after saying he would never do that. You can almost hear the shame in his tears that night, but when we read further, we don't see Jesus ambush him with condemnation; He met him on the beach with breakfast and forgiveness. He reinstated him, giving him a mission instead of a prison.

Shame wants to keep you in the ambush forever, but Jesus wants to pull you out and hand you back your orders.

In World War I, the story of the 'Lost Battalion' reminds me of the exact circumstances we are talking about here and they ultimately became a testament to grit, resolve, and unshakable leadership. In October 1918, roughly 554 men under the command of Major Charles Whittlesey found themselves cut off deep behind German lines in the Argonne Forest. No supplies. No reinforcements. No way out.

Surrounded on every side, they faced relentless attacks. German troops hammered them with machine gun fire and grenades. Hunger gnawed at their stomachs, thirst burned their throats, and exhaustion weighed on their bones. To make matters worse, their own American artillery, unaware of their position, began shelling them by mistake. Men were being killed by friendly fire.

No surprise but morale collapsed. Panic whispered through the ranks. Some soldiers believed surrender was the only option, but Major Whittlesey stood firm. He knew surrender wouldn't just cost them their freedom; it would cost them their honor, their legacy, and their mission. Instead, he ordered his men to dig in, hold fast, and refuse to give an inch.

Then came the moment of complete desperation. Whittlesey tied a message to a battered carrier pigeon named Cher Ami: "We are along the road parallel 276.4. Our artillery is dropping a barrage directly on us. For heaven's sake, stop it." The tiny bird flew through enemy fire, wounded but relentless, carrying hope in its wings and against all odds, the message got through. The shelling stopped.

For five brutal days, the Lost Battalion endured wave after wave of attack, holding strong, until reinforcements finally broke through. When the smoke cleared, only 194 of the original 554 men walked out alive. But they walked out with their heads high. They hadn't surrendered. They bore scars, yes, but they carried honor, not shame.

And here's the lesson I find in this for us: shame is its own battlefield. It's like being cut off behind enemy lines, surrounded by accusations, regrets, and lies. Shame whispers, "You failed. You're not enough. You'll never get out." It tells you surrender is your only option.

But Scripture calls us to fight differently. Psalm 3:3 reminds us, "But You, O Lord, are a shield around me, my glory, and the One who lifts my head." When the battle closes in, we don't wave the white flag, we send up the signal flare. We cry out to God in prayer. We dig into His Word. We call in the brothers who will stand shoulder-to-shoulder with us when we're pinned down.

You will most certainly walk out of some seasons scarred, but you don't have to walk out in shame. Like the Lost Battalion, you can emerge battered but unbroken, carrying honor, courage, and a testimony that God delivers those who refuse to quit.

Here's how the General teaches us to fight shame: Romans 8:1 says, "Therefore, there is now no condemnation for those who are in Christ Jesus." Condemnation is the enemy's weapon; Christ already disarmed it.

Isaiah 43:25 says, "I, even I, am He who blots out your transgressions, for my own sake, and remembers your sins no more." The General isn't keeping score against you.

2 Corinthians 5:17 says, "If anyone is in Christ, he is a new creation. The old has gone, the new has come." Shame tries to glue the old uniform back on you but ignore his tattered scraps, the General has already issued you new gear.

When you feel the ambush of shame, don't waste your strength arguing with it. Lies don't need debating; they need demolishing. And the weapon God has given you is His Word.

Deploy Scripture like calling in close air support. You don't have to fight shame in your own strength; you've got the power of heaven covering you. The moment you speak God's truth out loud, you're lighting up your position on the battlefield, calling in divine reinforcements that never miss their mark.

David said it this way in Psalm 34:4, "I sought the Lord, and He answered me; He delivered me from all my fears." When you send up that call through prayer, when you quote the promises of God, you can be confident that your coordinates are locked in and heaven hears you. The Father sees you and His response is never delayed or misplaced.

Shame will try to pin you down, whispering that you're forgotten and abandoned. But Scripture declares the opposite: "The Lord is near to the brokenhearted and saves those who are crushed in spirit" (Psalm 34:18). Every time you speak His Word, you're not just fighting back, you're declaring to the enemy and to your own soul, "Reinforcements are on the way."

Don't fight alone, call it in. Lean on the promises of God like a soldier trusts the sound of jets screaming overhead. When the smoke clears, you'll see what Scripture guarantees, "No weapon formed against you shall prosper" (Isaiah 54:17).

Drills & Practice

1. Name the Ambush: Write down the exact phrase shame uses against you. Be specific. Don't just write "I'm bad." Write the real ambush line: "I am a coward because I froze," or "I am unlovable because of what happened."
2. Call in Reinforcements: Share that shame with a trusted brother or sister in Christ. The ambush loses power when someone else sees it and stands with you. James 5:16 says confession brings healing for a reason.
3. Replace the Identity: Every time shame speaks, answer with Scripture about who you are in Christ. Don't just think it, say it out loud until your own ears believe it.
4. Build New Reflexes: Shame tries to hit the same place over and over again. Train yourself to respond instantly with truth,

the way a soldier dives for cover at the first crack of a rifle.

Thought & Discussion Questions

1. Have you noticed a difference between guilt and shame in your own life? Which one hits you harder?
2. What's one "ambush line" of shame that's been on repeat in your head?
3. How do you usually react when shame attacks? Retreat, fight, or freeze?
4. What Scripture speaks loudest against that specific shame?
5. Who in your life can be a reinforcement when shame ambushes you?

After Action Report & Mission Orders

1. Think back on this week. Where did shame ambush you? How did you respond? Did you use Scripture, or did you retreat?
2. Mission Orders: Choose one shame statement to confront head-on this week. Write it down. Counter it with one verse. Share it with one brother. And every time the ambush comes, fight back out loud.

Remember: shame may ambush you, but it doesn't own you. The General has already declared victory. Your job is to stand up, walk out of the forest, and keep fighting.

Chapter 6: The Stronghold of Fear – Advancing Against the Enemy

Let's be honest, most of us as warriors don't like to admit we have fear. We think saying it out loud makes us weaker. We put on the armor, grit our teeth, and convince ourselves that courage means never feeling afraid. But that's not courage, that's just denial and denial never wins battles.

Fear is one of the most powerful strongholds a soldier can face, not because it roars loudest, but because it often whispers the quietest. It doesn't always come charging like an enemy tank; sometimes it slips in like a sniper in the dark - silent, patient, deadly. It's that voice in the middle of the night that says:

"You cannot handle this."
"You're going to fail."
"You're not safe."
"You are alone."

And the longer you listen, the louder it gets.

Fear doesn't just attack your mind; it builds a fortress around your heart. It paralyzes your steps, telling you to stay huddled in the foxhole even when your General, the Commander of Heaven's Armies, has already ordered you to advance. It magnifies the threat and minimizes the presence of God. Left unchecked, fear becomes a fortified stronghold that keeps you trapped, ineffective, and convinced that victory is impossible.

But here's the truth: fear only has power when it goes unchallenged. The Bible says in 2 Timothy 1:7, *"For God has not given us a spirit of fear, but of power and of love and of a sound mind."* That means fear is not your inheritance. It's not your identity. And it's not your destiny.

Fear thrives in silence, but it dies in the light of God's Word. When you drag fear out into the open, speak Scripture over it, and submit it to Christ, you're cutting its supply lines. You're reminding your soul, and the enemy, that the battle doesn't belong to you; it belongs to the Lord (2 Chronicles 20:15).

So, this isn't about pretending you're fearless. It's about training your heart to trust more than you tremble. Courage isn't the absence of fear, it's moving forward even while your knees shake, knowing God goes before you. The foxhole feels safe, but you weren't called to hide. You were called to advance.

I was once honored to be able to walk through recovery with a man who had served faithfully overseas. His body had come home, but his mind was still stuck out there. Every sudden sound felt like the start of another firefight. He could not sit in a crowded restaurant without knowing the exits. His family saw him sitting at the table, but in his reality, he was still stuck on the battlefield.

When we talked, he admitted something that many men are afraid to say out loud. "I am not afraid of dying. I am afraid of living broken." That is the voice of fear. It tries to convince you that your best days are gone, that your mission is over, that you have no more strength to give.

But the General does not retire His soldiers. If you are still breathing, you are still enlisted.

The Bible doesn't gloss over fear, in fact many times it provides us very clear details. Joshua faced it before crossing into the Promised Land. David faced it on the run from Saul. Elijah faced it after Mount Carmel. And yet the General's command was the same each time: *"Do not be afraid, for I am with you."*

Joshua 1:9 says, *"Be strong and courageous. Do not be afraid. Do not be discouraged, for the Lord your God will be with you wherever you go."*

Psalm 27:1 says, *"The Lord is my light and my salvation. Whom shall I fear?"*

2 Timothy 1:7 says, *"God has not given us a spirit of fear, but of power and love and a sound mind."*

Fear will never leave on its own, you have to confront it with the truth of God's presence.

Consider the spring of 1940 when defeat seemed certain. Hitler's forces had torn through France like a wildfire, driving the British Expeditionary Force and their French allies to the edge of the continent. Over 400,000 Allied soldiers were trapped on the beaches of Dunkirk, hemmed in by the German army on land and pounded relentlessly from the air by the Luftwaffe. There was nowhere left to run.

The sea at their backs and the enemy before them, ammunition was running out and food was scarce. Every passing hour, German artillery crept closer and closer. Fear spread like a virus through the ranks and back in London, leaders began preparing for catastrophic loss, quietly bracing the nation for the unimaginable: hundreds of thousands of their sons would likely be slaughtered or captured.

But then... came what history calls "The Miracle of Dunkirk."

On May 26, under the shadow of annihilation, Britain launched Operation Dynamo, a desperate evacuation plan. But no one expected what would happen next. In one of the most extraordinary moments of World War II, hundreds of naval ships, merchant vessels, fishing boats, tugboats, yachts, and lifeboats, over 800 vessels in total, answered the call. Ordinary men and women, civilians with no training and no weapons, sailed straight into a warzone under fire to rescue soldiers who weren't even their own.

And something else happened, something no military strategist could explain. For reasons historians still debate, Hitler ordered his panzer divisions to halt their advance for three critical days. The weather shifted, giving cover from the Luftwaffe's bombardment. The English Channel, often treacherous, calmed like glass. Wave after wave, boat after boat, they crossed under fire and carried men home.

When it was over, more than 338,000 soldiers were pulled off those beaches. What had looked like certain defeat became a story of survival, courage, and impossible deliverance.

That moment can teach us something critical: fear tells you the story is already written. It whispers, "This is the end. You're surrounded. There's no way out." But fear doesn't get the final word, our General does. The Bible says, *"He makes wars cease to the ends of the earth"* (Psalm 46:9).

The battlefield of our minds is no different. The enemy may surround us with lies, shame, and regret. We may feel trapped, hemmed in with no escape. But when we call on our Commander, when we deploy Scripture like calling in reinforcements, heaven moves. What looks like the end can still become a victory when God intervenes.

Fear is not defeated by ignoring it or pretending it does not exist. Fear is defeated when you obey the General's orders despite it. Courage is not the absence of fear; courage is moving forward while fear screams at you to stop.

The process is simple, but not easy. Thoughts feed fear. Fear feeds feelings. Feelings feed actions. If you allow fearful thoughts to run unchecked, they will reinforce fearful feelings, and those feelings will dictate your actions. The only way forward is to break the chain at the thought level.

This is why Scripture repeats the command "Do not be afraid" over and over again. It is not a suggestion; it is a battle order. The General knows that if His soldiers obey that order, fear cannot control them.

Drills & Practice

1. Fear Inventory: Write down specific fears that ambush you during the week. Do not just write "I am anxious." Name the exact fear: "I am afraid my marriage will fail," or "I am afraid of what people think about me."
2. Scripture Counter: For each fear, find one verse that directly

confronts it. Post it somewhere you will see it daily. When the fear rises, speak that verse out loud.

3. Action Step: Pick one action this week that fear has been keeping you from doing. It could be calling a friend, attending a group, or praying out loud in front of others. Do it. Action breaks fear's stronghold.

Thought & Discussion Questions

1. What is one fear that feels like a stronghold in your life?
2. How has fear affected your actions, relationships, or faith?
3. Can you think of a time when you obeyed God even though you were afraid? What happened?
4. Which verse about fear do you need to commit to memory right now?
5. How can your brothers in Christ help you when fear tries to ambush you?

After Action Report & Mission Orders

1. Think back on a recent fear. Did you retreat, freeze, or advance? What thoughts fueled your fear, and how did you respond?
2. Mission Orders: Identify one fear this week. Name it. Counter it with Scripture. Take one action that fear has been blocking. And report back to your brothers.

Remember: Fear is loud, but it is a liar. The General has already declared that you are not abandoned. You are not outnumbered. You are not defeated. Your mission is still in motion. Advance.

Chapter 7: Isolation is the Kill Zone

A soldier never wanders off from his unit in the middle of a firefight because he knows better. Out there, alone, beyond the cover fire of his brothers, he becomes a silhouette against the chaos and an easy target for the enemy. That's why every soldier is trained to move together, cover each other, and never break formation. You break away, you get cut down.

The same principle is true in spiritual warfare. The battlefield may look different, but the danger is the same. Isolation is the kill zone. It's where the enemy sets his traps and waits with his sharpest weapons, not because you're weak, but because he knows you are most vulnerable when you are alone.

When you're separated from your brothers, when you slip away from the body, something shifts. The pressure feels heavier. The doubts grow louder. The whispers of shame, failure, and fear hit harder. Hope starts to dim. That's not random, that's strategy.

Satan has studied your patterns. He knows where you hesitate, where you're wounded, where you carry regret like a scar under the surface. He doesn't always need a direct assault. He knows that if he can divide you, he can conquer you. If he can separate you from your brothers, he can surround you without you even realizing it.

Isolation almost never begins with a loud declaration. It begins with a whisper. The enemy rarely storms the front gate of your mind; instead, he slips in through the cracks and plants lies that sound just close enough to truth to be believable.

He whispers: "Nobody understands you." And at first you nod, because it feels true.

He whispers: "You are too broken to be helped." And since you have seen your failures, you accept it.

He whispers: "They will think less of you if you share this." And since shame already weighs heavy, you keep silent.

The danger of these whispers is that they do not shout. They do not confront. They creep. They sneak in and reinforce themselves and once they take root, they grow into walls of isolation. I once read a story that reminded me of this being exactly how Satan attacks us:

The night was pitch-black except for the distant flicker of tracer fire. A small squad crouched low in a shallow ditch, clutching their rifles, waiting for the order to move. Then the radio cracked to life:

"Alpha Company, fall back immediately! You're surrounded! The entire right flank has collapsed!"

Panic ripped through the men. Some whispered curses under their breath; others tightened their grips on their weapons. Falling back meant abandoning the wounded. It meant retreating through open ground, straight into enemy fire. But the voice on the radio was frantic, urgent, believable.

Then their sergeant barked, "Hold your position! That's not our command frequency!"

Moments later, scouts returned with intel: the message had been fake, enemy propaganda broadcast on Allied channels, designed to trick them into exposing themselves to a real ambush. The "retreat order" wasn't an accident. It was psychological warfare, an enemy attempt to win the battle without firing a shot.

Satan fights exactly the same way and he's been using this tactic since the beginning. Jesus didn't mince words in John 8:44 when He called him "the father of lies." Lies aren't just part of his arsenal, they are his native tongue and he's a master craftsman, carefully shaping his attacks to strike where we're most vulnerable.

In Eden, he whispered to Eve: "Did God really say...?" (Genesis 3:1). One subtle question. One seed of doubt. And suddenly, paradise was poisoned.

In the wilderness, he came for Jesus Himself (Matthew 4:1–11). He quoted Scripture but twisted it. He offered shortcuts to glory, bypassing the cross. If Satan had the audacity to attack the Son of God with lies, he will absolutely come after you.

This is the enemy's strategy: flood the battlefield with misinformation. His whispers sound personal but they're tactical:

"You're too broken to be healed."
"God has abandoned you."
"This battle isn't worth fighting."
"You're already defeated, why even try?"

These aren't stray thoughts. These are precision strikes aimed at your identity, your faith, and your purpose.

We've seen this playbook used in real war. During World War II, the Allies used Operation Fortitude to deceive the Nazis before D-Day. They built a fake army, complete with inflatable tanks, dummy landing craft, and scripted radio chatter, to convince Hitler the invasion would happen at Pas-de-Calais instead of Normandy.

The ruse worked flawlessly. Hitler shifted his forces miles away from the real landing site, leaving Normandy vulnerable. By the time he realized the deception, it was too late, the beaches were taken, the foothold secured.

Victory began before the first shot was fired, in the battlefield of the mind.

Satan fights you the same way. He wants you to be convinced you're outnumbered, surrounded, and abandoned before you even lift your shield. But here's the truth: when you know the voice of your Commander, you can spot the enemy's propaganda for what it is, lies designed to break your will to fight.

That's why Paul reminds us in Ephesians 6:16 to *take up the shield of faith, with which you can extinguish all the flaming arrows of the evil one.* The arrows will come, but when you know your identity, your mission, and your Commander, they won't pierce your heart.

When the enemy isolates you, he takes away your reinforcements. He makes you believe you are alone in the fight, and once you believe that his attacks go unchecked. Left unchallenged, those whispers turn into chains: hopelessness, despair, bitterness, and eventually destruction.

Recognizing the whisper, that is truly the first step to breaking its power. You must learn to test every thought against the truth of Scripture. When the enemy says you are forgotten, you answer with Psalm 139: *"You hem me in, behind and before, and you lay your hand upon me."* When he says you are worthless, you answer with 1 Peter 2:9: *"You are a chosen people, a royal priesthood, a holy nation, God's special possession."*

You do not fight lies with feelings; you fight lies with truth.

Our General knows the enemy's tactics and is not surprised by his sneaky, conniving, and subversive attacks. That is why His orders are clear: Do not fight alone.

From the beginning, God recognized that isolation was not good. In Genesis 2:18 He said, *"It is not good for the man to be alone."* He wasn't talking just about marriage; he was referring to the human condition. We were made for connection.

Even in the design of His church, God wove brotherhood into the very foundation. Paul describes the church as a body in 1 Corinthians 12. No part can function on its own. The hand cannot say to the eye, "I do not need you." The foot cannot march without the leg. The body is designed to be interdependent.

Why? Because the General knows that brotherhood is not optional for survival, it is His battle strategy.

Brotherhood protects you when your guard is down, a brother sees what you cannot see, and he hears what you cannot hear. He can call out the enemy's lies in your life when you have grown deaf to them. Brotherhood strengthens you when your strength is gone. Look at Exodus 17:8-13 where Moses' arms grew tired in the battle against

Amalek, but Aaron and Hur stepped up to hold them up for Moses. The victory of Israel depended on that brotherhood.

Brotherhood also keeps you accountable as a man left unchecked will drift. He will compromise. He will rationalize his sin until it hardens into rebellion. But a brother who loves you enough to confront you will pull you back from the edge. Proverbs 27:6 reminds us, *"Faithful are the wounds of a friend, but deceitful are the kisses of an enemy."*

The General does not suggest brotherhood, He commands it. *"Encourage one another daily, as long as it is called 'Today,' so that none of you may be hardened by sin's deceitfulness"* (Hebrews 3:13). Encouragement is not a luxury; it is a safeguard. It's the difference between standing firm and falling apart.

When you stand with your brothers, you are a fortified wall. When you abandon formation though, you become a single stone, easily removed. The enemy knows this, which is why he fights so hard to keep you isolated. But the General has made it clear: your survival and your strength are found in community.

Brotherhood is not weakness. Brotherhood is power. It is the way men of God have always fought. David had his mighty men. Jesus had His disciples. Paul had Timothy, Silas, and Barnabas. Every great battle in Scripture was won not by lone warriors but by men who locked arms under the General's command.

So the order is clear. Stay in formation. Stay in brotherhood. Stand shoulder to shoulder. That is how we win.

Drills & Practice

1. Identify the Whispers – Write down the recurring lies you hear in your mind. Do not dress them up. Put them on paper. Once you see them written, you can start to confront them.
2. Answer with Truth – For every whisper, find a verse of Scripture that speaks directly against it. If the whisper is "You

are alone," your answer is Deuteronomy 31:6: "The Lord your God goes with you; He will never leave you nor forsake you."

3. Share with a Brother – Bring one of those whispers into the light by sharing it with someone you trust. Do not keep it locked inside. Lies lose their power when spoken aloud in the presence of truth and accountability.

4. Commit to Formation – Make a practical step this week to strengthen your brotherhood. That may be attending a men's group, calling a trusted friend, or reaching out to someone you know is struggling. Build your formation before the battle intensifies.

Thought & Discussion Questions

1. In what ways have you seen Satan use subtle lies or "psychological warfare" in your own life to make you doubt your identity, worth, or calling?

2. What circumstances, emotions, or patterns tend to make you withdraw from your brothers? How can you identify these triggers before the enemy exploits them?

3. When the enemy whispers lies, what is your first instinct—do you fight back with Scripture, stay silent, or retreat inward? How can you strengthen your response?

4. Think about a time when a brother "held up your arms" like Aaron and Hur did for Moses in Exodus 17:8–13. What did their support look like, and how did it impact the outcome?

5. Brotherhood isn't just about receiving help—it's about providing it. Who in your circle right now needs you to step in, encourage, or hold them up in prayer and accountability?

6. How do you currently discern between God's voice and the enemy's lies? What habits or spiritual disciplines help you stay aligned with your Commander's orders?

After Action Report & Mission Orders

1. Intel Debrief:

- The enemy's primary tactic is psychological warfare, lies disguised as truth, whispers aimed at your weak spots.
- Isolation is the kill zone. Alone, you're easier to target and harder to reinforce.
- Brotherhood is God's battle strategy. You were never meant to fight solo.

1. Battlefield Assessment:

- Enemy Strengths: Deception, division, doubt.
- Your Weapons: Scripture, brotherhood, prayer, accountability.
- Command Support: Psalm 18:2, Ephesians 6:16, Hebrews 3:13.

1. Immediate Mission Orders:

- Hold the Line: Stay connected with your brothers. No lone-wolf operations.
- Counter the Propaganda: For every lie whispered, deploy Scripture as your counter-strike.
- Call for Fire Support: Don't wait until you're pinned down, ask your brothers for prayer, accountability, and reinforcements.
- Advance in Formation: Strengthen your circle. Bring another man into the fight this week.

Remember: Stand firm. Lock shields. Hold the line. Your General's orders are clear: Do not fight alone.

Chapter 8: The Enemy's Trap: Spiritual Laziness

A soldier doesn't wait until the bullets start flying to learn how to fight. Armies drill daily because when chaos erupts, you won't rise to the level of your good intentions, you will fall to the level of your training. The battlefield doesn't reward wishful thinking; it exposes it.

And make no mistake, the enemy knows this. He doesn't always attack with a full-frontal assault. Sometimes his greatest tactic is far quieter and far deadlier: he lulls men to sleep.

It's not the roar of battle that takes most men out; it's the slow drift. He wants your guard lowered, your prayers faint, your discipline dulled. He doesn't need to destroy you with dramatic temptations if he can simply rock you into spiritual drowsiness. A distracted soldier is as vulnerable as a dead one.

That's why spiritual training matters. It's why Scripture calls us to *"be sober-minded; be watchful"* (1 Peter 5:8). The enemy doesn't mind if you're "religious," as long as you're passive. He doesn't care if you've heard the Commander's orders, as long as you're too spiritually tired to follow them.

And if you think you're immune to this, remember that even Jesus' closest disciples weren't.

The Garden of Gethsemane gives us one of the clearest warnings about spiritual laziness. It was the night of betrayal. Jesus was about to face His trial, suffering, and crucifixion. The fate of mankind hung in the balance, and He took His closest men with Him into the garden to pray.

"Sit here while I go over there and pray," He said to the disciples. Then He took Peter, James, and John deeper into the shadows. These were the same men who had stood with Him on the Mount of Transfiguration and seen His glory revealed. Now He asked them to

watch with Him in His darkest hour. He told them, "My soul is overwhelmed with sorrow to the point of death. Stay here and keep watch with me."

Jesus fell with His face to the ground, praying with such intensity that His sweat was like drops of blood. The Son of God was crying out in agony, fully aware of the weight of sin and the wrath of God that would be laid upon Him. And His brothers? They slept.

Three times Jesus returned to find them asleep. Three times He warned them, *"Watch and pray so that you will not fall into temptation. The spirit is willing, but the flesh is weak."*

That sentence describes every one of us. We want to be faithful...we want to stand strong...we want to honor Christ. But our flesh is weak. We get tired. We get distracted. We lose focus. The disciples' eyelids grew heavy that night, just like ours grow heavy when we should be on guard in prayer, in the Word, and in our obedience.

Yet notice something important. Jesus brought His brothers with Him. He did not isolate Himself in His struggle. He wanted them there. Brotherhood mattered, even though they failed Him. He modeled dependence, vulnerability, and the need for companionship in the battle. He showed us that even when our brothers fail us, God does not. Their sleep revealed human weakness while His prayer revealed divine strength.

The contrast in the garden is stunning. On one side, drowsy men succumbing to weakness. On the other side, the Son of God pressing through agony to embrace the Father's will. This is a mirror for us and question is, which side will we fall on?

Spiritual laziness is more dangerous than physical laziness because it doesn't just affect your body, it weakens your soul. It is when you stop caring enough to fight. The enemy doesn't usually tempt you with big, obvious sins first. Instead, he whispers small excuses:

"You can pray later."

"You already went to church this week, that should be enough."

"You can confess that sin another day."

"You're tired, God understands."

Those whispers sound harmless, but they are designed to dull your edge. Just as sleep overtook the disciples, distraction and comfort creep over us. Slowly we stop keeping watch. We miss opportunities to resist temptation. We leave doors open for the enemy to attack.

And when the trial comes, as it always does, we are unprepared.

In war, a sleeping soldier can cost a battle. In faith, a sleeping Christian can lose a war. Consider the early hours of December 16, 1944. The Ardennes Forest was silent, blanketed in fog and snow. American troops stationed along the front lines of what would become the Battle of the Bulge believed the German army was too weak and broken to launch any real counterattack. Many soldiers were cold, exhausted, and convinced they were safe.

But in the woods beyond, 200,000 German soldiers were silently gathering.

Under the cover of darkness, the Wehrmacht prepared one of the most ambitious surprise offensives of World War II. And when the attack came, it was brutal. Heavy artillery, tanks, and infantry units crashed through the forest. Whole sections of the Allied front collapsed within hours and not just because of German strength, but because many of the American soldiers who were on watch were caught unprepared or asleep.

General Eisenhower would later admit that U.S. intelligence and readiness had failed them. The assumption that the enemy was too beaten to fight back and that assumption left thousands of American soldiers vulnerable. Some units never had a chance to fire a shot before being overrun.

One small lapse, just a few hours of lowered guard, led to one of the bloodiest battles the U.S. Army has ever fought.

Jesus's command in the garden was simple: "Watch and pray." He was not giving them busywork to pass the time. He was preparing them. Prayer was the weapon. Watching was the discipline. Together they were the shield against temptation.

What the disciples failed to realize is the same thing many of us fail to realize: prayer is not optional in the battle. It is the battle. They wanted to fight for Him with swords when the soldiers came, but they could not fight for Him on their knees in the quiet of the garden.

That is the same mistake we so often make today. We want to rise up with bold actions when crisis strikes, but we neglect the quiet training of prayer that builds the strength to endure. The fight is always won on our knees before it is fought with our hands.

The Garden also shows us both the power and the limits of brotherhood. Jesus wanted His men with Him. He asked them to stay near. He valued their presence. That reminds us that we cannot go through the battle alone. We need brothers to walk with us, to encourage us, to help us stay awake and alert.

But it also shows us that no brother can carry the weight of your fight for you. They can stand beside you, but they cannot pray in your place. They can encourage you, but they cannot obey in your place. At some point every man must rise and go to the Father himself.

That balance is critical. Brotherhood is a gift. It gives us strength, encouragement, and accountability. But your ultimate source of strength must come from God. If you depend only on men, you will be disappointed. If you depend fully on God, you will never be abandoned.

The disciples' failure in the garden did not destroy the mission of Christ, but it did leave them unprepared for what came next. When the soldiers arrived, they panicked. Peter swung his sword in reckless anger.

The others ran away in fear. Their lack of preparation in prayer left them vulnerable in action.

That is the danger of spiritual laziness as it does not just affect your quiet time with God, it bleeds into your decisions, your relationships, your emotions, and your actions. Weakness in prayer leads to weakness in life.

The warning of Gethsemane is clear: if you sleep when you should be praying, you will stumble when you should be standing.

Drills & Practice

1. Watch & Pray Drill – Jesus' command in the garden was simple: "Watch and pray" (Matthew 26:41). Set aside three intentional prayer watches each day; morning, midday, and night.
    ◦ Morning: Start your day surrendering your plans to God and asking for strength to stand.
    ◦ Midday: Pause, reset, and ask the Holy Spirit to realign your thoughts and guard your heart.
    ◦ Night: Reflect on the battles of the day, confess where you fell short, and thank God for His grace.
    ◦ Purpose: Builds spiritual muscle memory so that prayer becomes a first response, not a last resort.
2. Scripture Readiness Drill – A soldier doesn't walk into combat without a loaded weapon. Neither should you.
    ◦ Choose five "battle verses" this week—Scriptures that remind you to stay alert and resist temptation (e.g., 1 Peter 5:8, James 4:7, Ephesians 6:10-18, Matthew 26:41, Psalm 119:11).
    ◦ Write them down on cards, your phone, or a journal.
    ◦ Review one verse in the morning, one at lunch, and one before bed.
    ◦ At the end of the week, test yourself. Can you quote

them? Can you explain why they matter?

- ○ Purpose: Fills your arsenal with truth so the enemy's whispers lose power.

3. Brotherhood Check Drill – You were not designed to fight alone. Even Jesus wanted His brothers near Him in the garden.
    - ○ Choose one or two men who will stand watch with you spiritually.
    - ○ Every week, ask three questions:
        - i. Where are you being tempted right now?
        - ii. How's your time in prayer and the Word?
        - iii. How can I pray for you and fight alongside you?
        - iv. Be honest. No masks. No excuses.
        - v. Purpose: Keeps you awake by staying connected. Accountability sharpens alertness and kills isolation.

4. Distraction Resistance Drill – The slow drift often happens because of subtle distractions.
    - ○ Identify your biggest "sleep triggers," the things that dull your edge:
        - i. Excessive scrolling
        - ii. Neglecting prayer
        - iii. Skipping fellowship
        - iv. Avoiding confession of sin
    - ○ Pick one distraction this week and declare war on it. Replace it with prayer, Scripture, or brotherhood time.
    - ○ Purpose: Weakens the enemy's foothold and trains you to respond with intentionality.

5. Endurance Under Fire Drill – This week, choose one 20-minute block of time to sit in silence before God. No

phone. No music. No distractions.

- Read a passage slowly (e.g., Psalm 46, John 15, Ephesians 6).
- Ask the Holy Spirit to speak and train your heart to listen.
- This discipline strengthens spiritual endurance, teaching you to focus when your flesh wants to quit.
- Purpose: Builds the stamina you'll need when real spiritual warfare comes.

6. Challenge for the Week – Set your alarm 15 minutes earlier tomorrow. Before your feet hit the floor, pray this: "Lord, keep me awake today. Open my eyes to the battles around me. Strengthen my hands to fight, sharpen my heart to obey, and keep me standing in Your strength, not mine."

- Then text one brother in your circle and ask him this:
  i. "Are you awake on the wall, or has the drift set in?"
  ii. Hold each other to it.

Thought & Discussion Questions

1. Where do you see spiritual laziness creeping into your life right now?
2. How do you identify the excuses the enemy whispers to keep you from prayer, scripture, or obedience?
3. In what ways have your brothers helped you stay awake in the fight? How can you strengthen those bonds further?
4. How does the story of the disciples in Gethsemane encourage or challenge you in your own walk with Christ?

After Action Report & Mission Orders

1. Reflect on your week. Were there moments where spiritual laziness overtook you? Did you miss opportunities to pray or to watch? What patterns do you see in your excuses? Write them down. Naming them takes away their power.
2. Mission Orders: Choose one drill you will commit to this week. It could be setting aside a set time for prayer, memorizing a verse, or journaling your reflections. Keep it specific, measurable, and daily.

Remember: The spirit is willing, but the flesh is weak. Your General has given the command: Watch and pray. Now it is time to obey.

Chapter 9: The Enemy's Trap - Pride

The deadliest ambush a soldier ever walks into is the one he brings on himself. Pride slips in disguised as strength, competence, and independence...until it's too late. No siren sounds when it arrives. No alarms flash. He simply stands a little taller, nods a little harder, breathes a little deeper, and suddenly, the walls of humility he once held collapse around him.

Take the story of General William Rupertus and the invasion of Peleliu in World War II. Despite warnings of brutal terrain and fierce resistance, Rupertus marched in confidently, proud of his Marines' reputation and spirit. In a pre-invasion speech, he promised the island would be secured in mere days, as if it were going to be a cakewalk and that confidence infected the division. But they encountered something else entirely: razor-sharp coral ridges, fortified Japanese defenses, and heat so oppressive it burned through the toughest resolve. What should have been a rapid victory turned into one of the bloodiest and costliest amphibious assaults in Marine Corps history and it was all fueled by pride that misread the mission's danger.

That is the trap, pride tells us we can handle anything. It blinds us to our need for preparation, for counsel, and for the endurance only God's strength provides. Before you know it, you're walking into the fight convinced you'll win...until you're bleeding under the weight of your own arrogance.

Because Satan doesn't need to lay siege to your life, he only needs to inflate your sense of self. Pride whispers: "You don't need help." "You're strong enough on your own." "You're wise enough without advice." And just like that, isolation becomes the kill zone.

Pride isn't just a sin, it's spiritual arrogance. It blinds us to our need for grace, brotherhood, and humility. And the most dangerous place to be is confident...without vigilance.

Heck, the very first rebellion in the universe was fueled by pride. Isaiah 14 and Ezekiel 28 describe how Satan, once a glorious angel, lifted his heart up in arrogance. He wanted to ascend above the throne of God, to be worshiped rather than to worship. Pride turned heaven's most beautiful servant into its greatest enemy.

The same poison dripped into Eden. The serpent told Eve that eating the fruit would make her "like God." Pride whispered, "You don't need to submit. You can be your own master."

Humanity has been choking on that same lie ever since.

For men, pride shows up in a thousand forms. It tells us we don't need help. It keeps us from admitting weakness. It convinces us that asking for prayer is weakness. It makes us nod along in Bible study, telling others we will be praying for them and want to support them, and all the while never confessing that we are struggling. Pride locks the lips and hardens the heart.

It can look like overconfidence too. How many fights in history have been lost because one man thought he was too strong to fail? Think of Peter, declaring to Jesus, *"Even if everyone else falls away, I never will."* Hours later, fear crushed his pride and he denied his Lord three times.

That is what pride does. It makes promises we cannot keep. It blinds us to our real need.

I wish I could tell you that pride was something I had only studied in Scripture and warned other men about, but the truth is, I've wrestled with it myself. Several years ago, our ministries began to grow rapidly. The number of men we were reaching was increasing, lives were being changed, and the requests for me to speak were multiplying faster than I could keep up with. Conferences, churches, retreats...I was being invited to share the mission God had placed on my heart, and doors I never imagined possible were opening one after another.

And here's the hard truth: I never once neglected God's calling, the mission, or the people we were serving. But somewhere along the way, pride quietly slipped through a side door I didn't even know was open. I started to believe, without ever saying it out loud, that maybe this growth was happening because of me; my passion, my words, my ability to connect with people on the stage.

I didn't realize it at the time, but I started craving the spotlight more than I craved the secret place with God. Speaking opportunities became fuel for my identity rather than fruit of His calling. I told myself I was serving faithfully, and in many ways, I was, but deep down, I was also feeding something dangerous.

Then came the moment that woke me up.

I had been booked to speak at a men's event at a church that I assumed would be packed. After all, the last few events had been standing room only. But when I arrived, there were less than ten men scattered in a room built for hundreds. I remember stepping onto that stage and feeling the silence press down like a weight. My jokes didn't land. My points didn't stir hearts. And for the first time in a long time, I walked off stage feeling empty.

That night, sitting alone in my car, God convicted me in a way I'll never forget. It wasn't loud. It wasn't angry. It was simple, piercing, and unshakable: "Todd, when did you start believing this was about you?"

I broke. Right there in that parking lot, I had my Jacob moment, wrestling with God until my pride was wounded enough to finally let go. I realized I had been relying on my gifts instead of the Giver, my stage instead of His strength.

The strange thing? Not long after that night, I noticed something powerful, when I humbled myself, sought His face above the platform, and stopped measuring success by applause, the ministry began to thrive again. God reminded me that the power was never in my words, it had always been in His Spirit.

That moment changed how I live and lead to this day. I set three rules for myself that I still follow with vigilance:

1. Stay on guard against pride. I keep watch over my heart daily, knowing that pride never charges the front gate, it always sneaks in quietly.
2. Speak to the one, not the crowd. Whether there are twenty people or two thousand, I've committed to stepping on every stage with one purpose: to speak faithfully to the person who needs the message, not to chase the applause of the masses.
3. Submit to accountability. I've shared my struggle with pride with a few trusted brothers who know me well. They ask the hard questions, call me out when I drift, and remind me who gets the glory.

Pride is the most silent sniper on the battlefield. You rarely see it coming. But when it takes its shot, it wounds your intimacy with God long before it takes down your influence with people.

Pride doesn't always shout, sometimes it whispers with subtlety:

"You're doing better than most men. You don't need to take this too seriously."

"If they knew your real struggles, they would reject you. Better to keep it quiet."

"Sure, you've got flaws, but not as bad as his. At least you're not like him."

Each whisper draws us away from humility. Each one sets us up for a fall. Proverbs warns that pride goes before destruction and a haughty spirit before a fall. Pride is not just a character flaw. It is a death sentence.

Jesus demonstrated the exact opposite spirit. He, who off all people could have puffed up with pride, had every right to claim glory, humbled Himself and took on the form of a servant. On the night of

His betrayal, He didn't strut around like a king, He knelt with a towel and washed His disciples' feet.

The Lord of the universe lowered Himself to the position of a slave. Why? To model the posture of true greatness. Jesus knew pride was the trap of the enemy, so He embodied humility as the weapon of heaven.

And He did not just model it. He commanded it: *"Whoever wants to be great among you must be your servant."* That is not weakness, that is strength under control.

History is littered with the wreckage of men who thought they were untouchable, men who believed their strength, wealth, or wisdom made them invincible. Scripture gives us some of the most sobering warnings about pride's power to destroy, and the stories are as raw today as when they were first written.

In Daniel 4, King Nebuchadnezzar stood atop the roof of his palace, gazing over the splendor of Babylon, the city of hanging gardens, golden temples, and unmatched power. His chest swelled as he declared, *"Is not this the great Babylon I have built by my mighty power and for the glory of my majesty?"*

Before the words were even out of his mouth, judgment fell. God stripped him of his throne, his sanity, and his dignity. The most powerful man on earth was driven into the wilderness like a wild animal, eating grass and sleeping under the dew of heaven. For seven long years, the man who once ruled nations couldn't even rule his own mind.

And yet, the moment Nebuchadnezzar lifted his eyes to heaven and finally acknowledged God's sovereignty, his sanity and kingdom were restored. His story reminds us that pride leads to humiliation, but humility leads to restoration.

Another reminder is King Uzziah who started out fairly well. 2 Chronicles 26 tells us he sought the Lord, and as long as he did, God gave him success. Under the king's leadership, Judah prospered, their armies grew, walls rose, and his fame spread far and wide.

But then came the turn. *"After Uzziah became powerful, his pride led to his downfall"* (2 Chronicles 26:16). Drunk on his own success, Uzziah marched into the temple to burn incense which was a role reserved for Levitical priests alone and by doing so, he blurred the God-ordained boundaries between kingship and priesthood. When confronted, the king became enraged and the text says he was "raging at the priests" while holding the censer in his hand.

In that moment, God struck him with leprosy. The king who once commanded armies, cities, and fortunes then lived in isolation, cut off from the temple and his people, dying in disgrace. His life screams this warning: the higher pride lifts you, the further the fall when God humbles you.

One more king to consider can be found in Acts 12 where King Herod Agrippa sat on his throne, dressed in royal robes, delivering a speech to the people. As he spoke, the crowd shouted, "This is the voice of a god, not a man!"

Herod didn't correct them. He didn't deflect the praise. He received it, like a man gorging himself on glory that wasn't his to claim. And immediately, Scripture says, *"an angel of the Lord struck him down because he did not give glory to God"* (Acts 12:23). He died, eaten by worms, his throne left empty.

Herod teaches us this: when pride convinces you to claim God's glory, you paint a target on your back. Pride whispers the same lies into every man's ear: "You've got this. You built this. You deserve this." But God's Word is clear: *"God opposes the proud but gives grace to the humble"* (James 4:6).

Pride is the ultimate battlefield trap as it blinds you, isolates you, and leads you straight into destruction. Humility, on the other hand, positions you under God's covering, where His strength sustains you and His grace lifts you up.

Pride also flourishes in isolation. Without brothers, there is no one to speak truth when arrogance begins to grow. But in real brotherhood, men can challenge each other. They can point out blind spots. They can hold up a mirror when pride starts whispering lies.

This is why James says to confess your sins to one another. Not so that we wallow in shame, but to disarm pride and walk in humility together. True brotherhood is one of God's greatest defenses against pride.

Drills & Practice

1. Practice confession. Speak your weaknesses out loud to trusted brothers. Humility grows where pride dies.
2. Serve intentionally. Look for ways to take the lower seat, to meet someone else's need, to wash feet instead of seeking applause.
3. Pray for humility. Ask God to show you where pride has crept in. He will answer that prayer.
4. Remember the cross. Nothing kills pride faster than remembering what it cost to save us.

Thought & Discussion Questions

1. Where has pride shown up in your life lately, and how did it affect your decisions or relationships?
2. Why is pride so dangerous to our walk with God, and why do you think the enemy uses it so often?
3. What specific examples from Jesus' life stand out to you as models of humility?
4. How can your brothers in Christ help you recognize and resist pride in your fight?

After Action Report & Mission Orders

1. Think about a time pride tripped you up.
   ◦ What lies did you believe?

- What was the result?
- How might humility and accountability have changed the outcome?

2. Mission Orders: This week, choose one intentional act of humility. Serve someone without recognition. Confess a weakness to a brother. Refuse to let pride dictate your steps.

Remember: The enemy's trap is pride, but the weapon of heaven is humility. Walk in it.

Chapter 10: The Enemy's Trap – Compromise

It was April 18, 2008, at a remote outpost in the mountains. The mission was simple, hold the line. For weeks the enemy tested the perimeter...a single rifle shot at dusk...footprints just outside the wire...a faint radio echo that did not belong. Each time the platoon pushed back, then slowly the routines slipped. A gate was left unlatched because someone would be right back. A watch rotation was shortened because everyone was tired. A weapons check was skipped because nothing had happened in days.

Before dawn the ridge lit up from fire from the high ground and fighters poured down in waves. The men fought hard, but the enemy had mapped every weakness and walked through the doors that had been left open. At a glance, this looked like a fluke, but the reality is the post did not fall in one night. It fell one small shortcut at a time.

That is how compromise works. Not with a crash, but with a quiet click. Not with a charge, but with a slow drift.

Our enemy is not random; he is patient and strategic. Most men do not wake up and decide to wreck a marriage, abandon faith, and torch a reputation. The trap is set one inch at a time. It starts with a joke that crosses the line or with prayer skipped for a day, then two, then a week. It starts with a late night click that pretends to be relief or with one more shift that makes Sunday feel optional. Alone, each of these feels small. Together, they eat the house from underneath.

Scripture has a name for this pattern. *"Catch for us the foxes, the little foxes that ruin the vineyards"* (Song of Solomon 2:15). Foxes do not rip down full vines, they slip in and gnaw young growth so the harvest never comes. Jesus said He is the vine and we are the branches, and the Father desires much fruit in us (John 15). If the foxes live in the fence line, fruit withers and witness fades.

I, like so many others, have had my own stumbles with compromise. I tend to laugh and joke around a lot, and it's easy for me to slide back into the type of jokes and playful comments that I once thought were perfectly fine. But now, as a follower of Jesus, I know they're borderline at best and often just inappropriate. Those compromises haven't just been words, they've led to hurt feelings, damaged relationships, and moments where my testimony was weakened instead of strengthened. That's a "little fox" at work. Seemingly small, but capable of wrecking the vineyard of what God is trying to grow in and through me.

We have to ask, where does compromise come from and why do we fall for it? Compromise usually grows in four soils of the heart. Many veterans will recognize these pressures because of trauma, hyper alertness, and exhaustion press on each and every one.

Comfort. We crave easy. Scripture takes focus, prayer takes persistence, obedience takes effort. Compromise will whisper to us, "Relax, you earned it." The easy path though erodes our muscle.

Fear. We fear what people think. We stay quiet when crude or inappropriate talk rolls through the room. We hide our Bible at work. The fear of man lays a snare, but whoever trusts the Lord is safe (Proverbs 29:25).

Desire. Lust, greed, pride, appetite. Desire unchecked rewrites truth. James writes that desire conceives and gives birth to sin, and sin when it is full grown gives birth to death (James 1:14 to 15).

Weariness. Tired men lower their guard. Veterans know the drag of long nights, soul fatigue, and triggers that come without warning. Galatians 6:9 calls us to not grow weary in doing good, because the harvest comes to those who do not give up.

The enemy lies into each of those types of soil. It is not a big deal. No one will know. Everyone does it. You deserve this. Small cracks become breaches. Breaches ultimately become collapse.

Look at Samson, who perfectly showed us the slow leaks before the collapse (Judges 13 to 16). Samson did not fall in one night with Delilah. He touched what he vowed to avoid, chased what God forbid, mocked the enemy for sport, and ignored counsel. Step by step, he traded consecration for convenience. By the time he slept in Delilah's lap, he had already cut his own strength by inches.

What about Saul who demonstrated partial obedience that felt religious (1 Samuel 15). God's command was clear, but Saul spared what God said to destroy, then dressed it up as sacrifice. Samuel said, to obey is better than sacrifice. Half obedience is disobedience with church clothes on.

Then we see David lingering when he should have looked away (2 Samuel 11). David stayed home when kings went to war. He saw, then lingered. Lingering became sending, sending became taking, and soon the man after God's heart carried blood on his hands. It began with a look that stayed too long.

Each of these stories shows the same drift. Compromise doesn't shout, it whispers. It moves the line a little, then a little more, and just keeps going without us ever noticing.

The Lord, our general, has made His orders for us clear. *"Be holy, because I am holy"* (1 Peter 1:16). He never gives us commands without supply though and in this He gives His Spirit for power, His Word for clarity, and His people for protection.

Guard the line by knowing the Scriptures and in doing so you can spot a fox the moment it moves. Guard the line by linking arms with brothers who ask hard questions and give real help. Guard the line by prayer that keeps your heart awake to God. Guard the line by fast confession and real repentance so breaches are sealed before the enemy pours through.

Unfortunately, far too many Christians forget that we are called to do all of this...in love. We never excuse sin, but we never forget the person. Speak the truth in love as Ephesians 4:15 commands. Restore gently as Galatians 6:1 commands. Aim not at winning an argument, but at winning a brother back to the Shepherd who changes hearts from the inside out.

Drills & Practice

1. Perimeter check. Walk the fence line of your life with God this week. Ask, where have I moved the line. Name three small compromises that recur. Write them down. Pray Psalm 139:23-24 over each one.

2. SLLS for the soul. Field craft teaches stop, look, listen, smell. Do the same twice a day for five minutes. Stop what you are doing. Look at what you are letting in through your eyes. Listen to the thoughts you are agreeing with. Smell for the smoke of temptation before the fire starts. Reset with Philippians 4:8.

3. Truth cards. Pick four lies that feed your compromise. Pair each with a verse. Example, I am alone is answered by Deuteronomy 31:6. Keep these cards on your phone and in your wallet. Read them morning and night.

4. Tripwire partners. Choose two brothers. Tell them your specific foxes. Give them permission to text you unannounced and ask for a short report. You answer with three words, tempted, resisted, or fell. Keep it simple, honest, and fast.

5. Replace, do not just remove. Name one habit you will replace this week. Replace twenty minutes of late night scrolling with twenty minutes in the Psalms. Replace a crude chat with a call to pray with a brother. Ephesians 4 teaches put off and put on. Do both.

6. HALT check. Before a known trigger time ask, am I hungry, angry, lonely, or tired. If yes, delay decisions. Eat, breathe, reach out, rest, then choose.

7. Immediate confession protocol. If you cross a line, confess to God at once, then to a brother within twenty four hours. Read 1 John 1:9 out loud. Close with Psalm 51:10.

Thoughts & Discussion Questions

1. Where have little foxes already slipped inside your fence? What fruit has suffered?
2. Which soil grows compromise most in you, comfort, fear, desire, or weariness? What Scripture speaks directly to that soil?
3. For veterans, how do triggers or numbness push you toward small compromises? What plan can your brothers help you set for those moments?
4. In Samson, Saul, or David, what warning lands most clearly for you and why?
5. Where have jokes, words, or sarcasm hurt your witness? What amends or apologies would honor Christ?
6. What three guardrails could you install this week to protect your eyes, time, and relationships?

After Action Report & Mission Orders

1. Situation: The enemy prefers quiet breaches. Compromise enters through small doors and grows until walls fail.
2. Mission: Guard the vineyard God has entrusted to you. Chase out the foxes. Hold the line in love and truth.
3. Execution: Command and signal. Daily prayer watches morning, midday, night. Scripture in hand. Truth cards ready.
4. Support: Tripwire partners set and informed. Weekly check in on known trigger times.
5. Actions on contact: When tempted, halt, quote your paired verse, text your brother, remove yourself from the scene, pray

for two minutes out loud.

6. Recovery: If you fall, confess fast, repent clearly, repair the relationship where needed, reset the guard.

Remember: Hold the line. Chase out the foxes. Stay close to the Vine. Your life, your witness, and your brothers are worth it.

Chapter 11: The General's Orders – Living Under Christ's Command

Every soldier knows that his strength doesn't come from deciding his own plan but from following the orders of his commanding officer. A soldier who chooses to fight his own war, in his own way, quickly finds himself cut off, exposed, and defeated. The Christian life is no different. We aren't free agents wandering through life hoping things turn out okay. We are soldiers under command, enlisted into the service of the greatest General who has ever lived, Jesus Christ.

Paul captures this truth when he writes in 2 Timothy 2:4, *"No soldier gets entangled in civilian pursuits, since his aim is to please the one who enlisted him."* That verse is both sobering and liberating. It reminds us that our lives aren't about chasing comfort, success, or approval. Our aim is singular and clear: to please the One who called us into His army. The moment we forget that we open ourselves up to confusion and defeat.

But here's what makes Christ's command different from any earthly general: His orders are never cruel, manipulative, or self-serving. They are born out of love and aim at our good. When He says, *"Take my yoke upon you and learn from me, for I am gentle and humble in heart, and you will find rest for your souls"* (Matthew 11:29), He's telling us that obedience to Him isn't a crushing burden...it's freedom. He commands because He knows what we need better than we do. He directs because He sees the battlefield far more clearly than we ever could.

A friend of mine once told me a story from his time in the Iraq War during 2004. His team of U.S. soldiers were stationed in the city of Fallujah where the streets were always so unpredictable, sometimes quiet and other times erupting with sudden chaos. On this occasion his team had been ordered to hold position on a critical intersection that really didn't look like much, just a dusty road with a few crumbling buildings, but it was a key supply line for the unit's mission.

Hours passed without incident, and the soldiers grew restless. One young soldier suggested they move forward and scout the next block as he had reasoned that sitting in one place was making them a target. His temptation to act on instinct was strong but the platoon leader reminded the whole team of their orders: "Hold this ground. Reinforcements are counting on us to keep this position secure."

Moments later, an enemy ambush erupted just beyond them on the very block the young soldier had suggested moving into. RPGs and small arms fire lit up the night and if the platoon had abandoned their post and wandered ahead, they would have been caught in the kill zone with no cover and no backup. Instead, because they obeyed their order to hold, they provided covering fire, protected supply routes, and ultimately saved lives.

That night is burned into my friend's memory as a lesson that obedience is not weakness, it's strength. Orders aren't given to limit a soldier's freedom but to preserve it, to protect the mission, and to ensure survival.

Our Christian life mirrors that moment as we many times may not always understand why Christ commands what He does. Sometimes His orders feel slow, uncomfortable, or even restrictive. But He sees the ambushes waiting just around the corner that we are unable to recognize. His commands are not about limiting us; they are about leading us into life.

The enemy hates when we walk in obedience as he knows that if we stay under Christ's orders, we walk in strength, clarity, and protection. So, he does everything he can to lure us away. Sometimes he whispers that we should follow our own heart, that we can be our own masters. Sometimes he pushes us to blend in with the culture, to "go with the flow" so we don't stand out. Other times he tempts us with partial obedience, convincing us that halfway is good enough. But in the end, each of these paths leads to the same place: bondage, regret, and spiritual defeat.

So how do we live under Christ's orders in the real, everyday moments of life?

We stay close to His voice. A soldier who refuses to read the field manual or listen to the radio transmission from his commander is headed for disaster. For us, that means staying rooted in God's Word and cultivating a prayer life that listens as much as it speaks.

We trust His authority. Soldiers don't get to debate every command. They obey because they know their commander sees the bigger picture. In the same way, Christ knows the traps hidden ahead, the weak spots in our defenses, and the schemes of the enemy before they're even set in motion. Obedience is not blind; it's trusting His vision.

We stay with our unit. No soldier was ever meant to fight alone. Walking under orders means staying in fellowship with other believers, encouraging one another to keep the mission in view and not drift into civilian distractions.

Obedience, then, is not about lifeless rule-keeping, it's about trust. It's believing that when Christ commands, He does so out of love and with a vision we don't have.

I remember a season in my life when I was running hard after success. I had all the plans mapped out with my exact career steps, financial goals, even ministry goals that looked good on paper. But I wasn't listening for Christ's orders. I was charging forward into enemy territory without checking in with my General.

It didn't take long before I found myself excelling in what the world calls success with money, toys, cars, and homes but I found myself spiritually exhausted, cut off from my brothers, and wondering why everything felt so empty. The turning point came when I realized I had been trying to live the Christian life like a freelancer instead of a soldier under command.

When I got back into the Word, slowed down to actually listen to Christ's leading, and surrounded myself with brothers who kept me accountable, things changed. Did my life instantly get easier? No. But it got aligned. I wasn't chasing my own glory or temporary items anymore; I was moving in step with Christ's command. And that alignment brought peace, clarity, and strength I hadn't known in years.

Drills & Practice

1. Morning Roll Call – Before you check your phone, check in with your Commander. Pray "Lord, what orders do You have for me today?"
2. Weapons Maintenance – A good soldier cleans his rifle daily so in these matters you maintain your faith weapon by staying in Scripture daily. Read, reflect, and apply, even if it's just one verse you carry into the day.
3. Radio Check – Soldiers test communication regularly. Spend a few minutes in silence during the day simply listening to God. No agenda, no requests, just listening.
4. Unit Formation – Stay connected to your brothers. Commit to a men's group, Bible study, or accountability partner where you can encourage and be encouraged.

Thoughts & Discussion Questions

1. Why do you think obedience often feels like a restriction instead of freedom?
2. In what areas of your life do you tend to "freelance" instead of following Christ's orders?
3. How does Christ's leadership differ from the leadership styles we see in the world?
4. What daily "drills" could you begin to practice this week to stay under His command?
5. Share with a brother about a time when obedience to Christ

led you to unexpected blessing or protection.

After Action Report & Mission Orders

1. What was the mission? To understand the importance of living under Christ's command as our General.
2. What actually happened? We saw that obedience brings freedom, protection, and strength, while disobedience brings confusion and defeat.
3. Why does it matter? Because the Christian life is not about surviving, it's about advancing under orders from the One who already secured the victory.
4. Mission Orders for the Week:
    ◦ Begin each day with "Morning Roll Call" asking Christ for His orders before starting your day.
    ◦ Identify one area where you've been "freelancing" and surrender it to His command.
    ◦ Share with a brother in Christ the mission you're committing to and ask him to check in with you by week's end.

Remember: The Christian man is not called to drift through life making it up as he goes. He is a soldier under command and the beauty of this truth is that our General is not a tyrant demanding our sacrifice from a safe distance. He is a Savior who has already laid down His life for the troops. He has already gone ahead of us into the fight and secured the victory. Now He calls us to trust Him, follow Him, and live under His command. Brothers, let us be men who obey, not out of fear, not out of legalism, but out of love for the One who has never led us astray.

Chapter 12: The Armor of God - The Belt and Breastplate

You don't put on armor when life feels safe, you put on armor when there's a war. And make no mistake about your current situation, you are in one.

This isn't a war fought with bullets and bombs, but it's just as deadly. Every day, you wake up on a battlefield where unseen forces are fighting for control of your mind, your heart, and your soul. The Apostle Paul didn't use military language in Ephesians 6 because it sounded cool, he used it because he understood the stakes. He knew the Christian life isn't a playground; it's a warzone.

Some days, the attacks are obvious with temptation, anger, lust, addiction, shame, while other days, the hits are subtle in the form of discouragement, doubt, compromise, and distractions designed to slowly pull you away from God's mission for your life. The enemy doesn't take days off and he's not shooting warning shots.

That's why Paul commands us to *put on the full armor of God, so that you can take your stand against the devil's schemes* (Ephesians 6:11). Armor isn't optional. You don't stumble into victory; you prepare and suit up for it.

When Paul wrote to the church in Ephesus, his readers didn't have to try and imagine the sight of a Roman soldier, they saw them daily. Ephesus was a major port city in Asia Minor, a hub of commerce, culture, and politics, but it was also a city under the heavy hand of Roman control. Soldiers from the elite Roman legions patrolled the streets, their presence constant and unignorable.

These weren't casual guards; they were the most disciplined and battle-hardened warriors of their age, trained from youth in the art of war. Every citizen and merchant knew the authority behind the glinting armor, the short stabbing gladius at their side, and the eagle standards they carried that represented the power of Caesar himself.

To the common people, Roman soldiers were both protectors and oppressors as they enforced Rome's laws with an iron fist and any resistance was crushed swiftly and brutally. Their intimidation was a weapon as sharp as any sword they carried. Their polished helmets, broad shields, and layered breastplates were meant to do more than protect, they projected dominance. If a soldier knocked on your door, you answered. If one spoke, you listened. And if a unit marched through the streets in full formation, every shopkeeper and child stepped aside in silence.

For believers in Ephesus, seeing these soldiers was a daily reminder of earthly power, and yet Paul pointed them beyond it, to a different kind of armor, forged not from steel but from faith, righteousness, and truth. Paul understood what his audience in Ephesus would picture immediately: the hardened Roman soldiers who patrolled the streets. Battle-tested. Fearless. Uncompromising. These soldiers didn't survive by accident; they survived because they were prepared. Every piece of their armor served a purpose, and missing even one left them vulnerable to defeat.

Your fight is no different. If you try to face the battles of life unprotected, you're walking into the kill zone unarmed. But God hasn't left you defenseless. He's given you spiritual armor designed to withstand every scheme, every attack, every ambush from the enemy, but it is your responsibility to put it on.

The first piece that Paul begins with is the foundation on which the rest of the armor depends, the belt of truth. In Roman times, a soldier's belt wasn't just a piece of leather to keep his tunic from flapping around. It was the foundational piece of his entire armor. The belt gathered his garments so he could move freely, and it held the sword, the dagger, and other essential gear. Without it, the rest of the armor felt loose and unsteady. The soldier wasn't ready for battle until his belt was strapped on tight.

Spiritually, the belt of truth serves the same purpose as truth is what holds everything else together. Without truth, righteousness becomes subjective, faith becomes shaky, and salvation feels uncertain. Jesus said in John 8:32, *"You will know the truth, and the truth will set you free."* Truth is not just a concept, it is a Person. Jesus Himself declared in John 14:6, *"I am the way, the truth, and the life."* When we fasten the belt of truth around our lives, we are choosing to live anchored in Him.

Truth is what gives us freedom of movement in life. Without it, we are tangled up in lies, weighed down by confusion, and vulnerable to deception. Satan is called the *"father of lies"* in John 8:44, and his main weapon has always been deception. From the Garden of Eden until now, his tactic is to twist, distort, and confuse the truth so that we lose confidence in God's Word. But the belt of truth gives us clarity, stability, and readiness. It allows us to stand firm in a world full of shifting values and distorted narratives.

Truth also secures us in our identity. So many of us walk around unsure of who we really are. The lies of culture tell us that our worth is in our success, our strength, or our possessions, but when we have the belt of truth buckled, it reminds us that our identity is in Christ alone. It holds us together when the world tries to pull us apart.

The belt can be absolutely critical to battles as we saw during World War II when soldiers often carried far more than just weapons into battle. Their belts were the anchor point for their canteens, ammunition pouches, grenades, bayonets, first-aid kits, and sometimes even rations. Veterans from that war that I have spoken to have plainly told me, "If you lost your belt, you lost your fight."

One of the stories I distinctly remember was regarding the brutal fighting in the Battle of the Bulge in December 1944. American troops faced freezing conditions, surprise German offensives, and chaotic combat. Many soldiers recalled that in the scramble of battle, if a man's belt snapped or was lost, his equipment scattered. Suddenly, he was slowed down, he had no ammo at hand, no canteen, and no gear to survive the cold. Some soldiers survived the fight not because they were the strongest, but because their belt held firm under pressure, keeping everything else in place when chaos erupted.

One heroic vet told me that it was part of his routine to always ensure he had inspected his belt and then secured it properly. By always ensuring he had his belt he said could reload faster, move more freely, and carry on in the thick of combat. His belt wasn't flashy like a rifle, but he felt it was the difference between being ready or being exposed.

That's exactly why Paul began with the belt of truth. Without it, the rest of your spiritual equipment scatters. But when you've strapped on God's truth, you're ready to move, endure, and fight effectively no matter what chaos hits.

Right alongside the belt comes the breastplate of righteousness. For a Roman soldier, the breastplate was critical as it covered the chest and protected the heart and lungs, those vital organs that sustain our lives. A well-made breastplate many times meant the difference between life and death in close combat.

Spiritually, righteousness functions as our breastplate. Righteousness is not about being perfect on our own; it is about being covered by Christ's righteousness. 2 Corinthians 5:21 tells us, *"God made him who had no sin to be sin for us, so that in him we might become the righteousness of God."* That means when the enemy hurls accusations, when shame tries to take hold, and when guilt threatens to paralyze us, we are protected by the righteousness of Christ.

That's right, the righteousness of Christ, as our righteousness is not our own. Isaiah 64:6 says that our righteous acts are like filthy rags before God. Left to ourselves, we have no protection. But in Christ, our hearts are shielded and His righteousness deflects the attacks of condemnation, keeping us standing when shame or temptation tries to pierce us.

The breastplate also reminds us to guard our hearts in daily life. Proverbs 4:23 tells us, *"Above all else, guard your heart, for everything you do flows from it."* What you let into your heart will determine your direction. The music you listen to, the conversations you entertain, the thoughts you dwell on, these all affect the condition of your heart. The breastplate of righteousness is both a gift and a responsibility. God gives us His righteousness, but we must also choose to walk in holiness, keeping our hearts pure and devoted to Him.

I can remember seasons in my life when I wasn't wearing the belt of truth very tightly. I allowed half-truths and cultural lies to seep into my thinking. When I wasn't grounded in God's truth, my identity felt shaky, my confidence in prayer wavered, and I was more easily swayed by temptation. But the more I intentionally strapped on truth through reading Scripture, speaking it out loud, and surrounding myself with brothers who reminded me of it, the steadier I became.

The breastplate of righteousness also became personal for me in those same seasons. There were times when the enemy whispered accusations: "You're not worthy. You've failed too many times. You'll never get it right." If I had to stand on my own righteousness, he would have been right. But because I stand covered in Christ's righteousness, those accusations bounced off. My heart was guarded not by my performance but by His finished work on the cross.

Because that's the truth we have to settle deep in our souls: the battle isn't won by how perfectly we perform but by how firmly we stand in what Christ has already done. The enemy will keep firing his accusations, but we don't fight for victory, we fight from it. And once you learn to walk covered in His righteousness, you begin to see every other piece of the armor differently. The belt. The breastplate. The shield. The sword. Each one becomes more than a metaphor; they become your lifeline on the battlefield. And in the next chapter, we're going to pick up the next piece of that armor, because the fight isn't slowing down, and neither can we.

Drills & Practice

1. Strap on the Belt of Truth Daily: Begin each morning with one declaration of God's truth. For example, say out loud, "I am a child of God. I am forgiven. I am free." Let truth be the first thing you put on each day.
2. Guard the Heart with the Breastplate: Throughout the day, ask yourself: "Is what I'm letting into my heart pure, holy, and pleasing to God?" If not, take action to protect your heart.
3. Combat Lies with Scripture: Write down three lies you've been tempted to believe and find a specific Scripture verse that speaks God's truth against each one. Whenever that lie arises, repeat the verse as a counterattack.

Thoughts & Discussion Questions

1. What are some lies that you have believed in the past that made you vulnerable in your faith?
2. How does living in the truth of Jesus give you freedom compared to living in half-truths or cultural definitions?
3. What practical steps can you take to guard your heart each day from influences that weaken your walk with God?
4. How can we as brothers help one another strap on truth and walk in righteousness?

After Action Report & Mission Orders

1. What went right? Did you begin your day with truth? Did you feel more secure and steady in your faith as a result?
2. What went wrong? Where did lies or shame sneak in to weaken your confidence? Did you leave your heart unguarded in any area?

3. How do we improve? Commit to strapping on the belt and breastplate daily. Share with a brother one area where you struggle to believe the truth or guard your heart, and allow him to walk with you in accountability.
4. Mission Orders: Each day this week, declare truth over your life and guard your heart with Christ's righteousness. Keep the belt tight and the breastplate secure.

Remember: The battle is won not by your strength but by standing firm in His truth and His righteousness.

Chapter 13: The Armor of God - The Shoes and Shield

Paul continues his description of the armor with footwear and as a lifelong sneakerhead, I think these should be at the top of the list. At first glance, shoes might not seem as critical as a sword or shield, but for a soldier of those times, proper footwear meant survival. Roman legionaries wore studded sandals called caligae. These weren't flimsy flip-flops like we see in old movies, they had thick soles, reinforced straps, and small hobnails driven into the bottom like cleats. They gave soldiers stability in rough terrain and traction in close combat. With the right shoes, soldiers could march for miles, stand firm on uneven ground, and hold their line without slipping.

Paul says in Ephesians 6:15, *"and with your feet fitted with the readiness that comes from the gospel of peace."* Notice he connects footwear with readiness. The gospel gives us peace with God (Romans 5:1), and that peace equips us to stand firm. No matter how the ground shifts beneath us, we are anchored.

I have found that just like most other instances in scripture, peace here doesn't mean the absence of conflict, it means inner stability and confidence in God, even when the world rages. Just like a Roman soldier's hobnailed sandals dug into the dirt to hold their ground, the peace of the gospel digs into our hearts and keeps us from being pushed back by fear, anxiety, or chaos.

But these shoes also allow for mobility. The gospel is not just defensive; it is also offensive. Isaiah 52:7 says, *"How beautiful on the mountains are the feet of those who bring good news, who proclaim peace, who bring good tidings, who proclaim salvation."* The soldier of Christ is not meant to sit still. He moves forward with the gospel, carrying it into enemy territory, announcing the victory of Christ.

We have seen all through history it demonstrated the importance of soldiers' footwear time and again. During Napoleon's disastrous retreat from Russia in 1812, thousands of French soldiers froze and collapsed and not because of bullets, but because of their feet. Many had boots that wore out during the 500-mile march through snow and ice and without proper footwear, frostbite, infection, and exhaustion decimated the army more than enemy fire ever did. By contrast, armies that marched with durable footwear could endure longer, maneuver better, and keep fighting when others fell.

Paul's imagery for us is clear, without spiritual shoes, you won't last long in this fight. You will slip, stumble, or collapse under pressure. But when your feet are fitted with the readiness of the gospel of peace, you can march forward no matter how treacherous the ground.

Next comes the shield of faith. Roman shields (scutum) were not the small round plates we often imagine or see in the old black and white movies. They were large, rectangular shields, about four feet tall and two-and-a-half feet wide, curved to cover the whole body. They were made of layered wood and covered in leather, and they could be soaked in water before battle to extinguish flaming arrows.

Paul writes in Ephesians 6:16, *"In addition to all this, take up the shield of faith, with which you can extinguish all the flaming arrows of the evil one."* The enemy's arrows are lies, temptations, accusations, and doubts, all lit with fire to cause maximum damage. But when faith is raised, those fiery attacks are quenched.

The faith that Paul is referencing here is not blind optimism, it is trust in the promises of God. Hebrews 11:1 reminds us, *"Now faith is confidence in what we hope for and assurance about what we do not see."* Faith says, "I may not see the answer yet, but I trust the One who holds it." When the enemy whispers, "God has abandoned you," faith raises the shield and replies, *"Never will He leave me, never will He forsake me"* (Hebrews 13:5).

Even more powerful was the Roman tactic called the testudo ("tortoise" formation). Soldiers interlocked their shields side by side and overhead, creating an impenetrable wall that went all the way around and over the top of their formation. Flaming arrows bounced off harmlessly, and the army advanced together. Likewise, our faith is strongest in community. When brothers lock shields, standing shoulder to shoulder, the attacks of the enemy cannot break through.

I have had far too many times in my life when the ground beneath me felt unstable, circumstances shifting like sand. Anxiety and fear pulling me down and drowning me in despair, but in those times when I remembered the peace of the gospel, I could stand. Even when the storm raged, I was anchored in Christ.

And when the enemy's arrows came, those arrows of doubt, shame, and fear, it was faith that shielded me. Not faith in myself because far too often it was plainly obvious that I was not enough to handle my circumstances, but rather faith in God's promises. I remember seasons where the only thing I could do was cling to a verse, repeating it like a battle cry. Each time I did, it was as though I was soaking my shield, extinguishing those arrows one by one.

The shield can stop the arrows, but make no mistake, the enemy won't stop firing. His attacks will keep coming, and some will strike closer than you expect. That's why we can't stop at defense, we need to go on the offensive. Faith gives us the courage to stand, but the next piece of armor gives us the weapon to advance. In the next chapter, we're picking up the sword, the Word of God, and learning how to wield it like a warrior, because surviving the battlefield isn't enough. We're called to overcome.

Drill and Practice

1. Put on the Shoes Daily: Each morning, pray: "Lord, help me stand in Your peace today, and help me carry Your gospel wherever You send me."

2. Strengthen the Shield: Write down three promises of God from Scripture and commit them to memory. When doubt or temptation strikes, raise those promises like a shield.
3. Link Shields with Brothers: Identify one or two men you can lock arms with in faith. Commit to praying for each other and standing together against spiritual attacks.

Thoughts & Discussion Questions

1. What situations in your life make it hard to "stand firm"? How does the gospel of peace anchor you in those times?
2. What "flaming arrows" of the enemy do you most often face (temptation, doubt, shame, fear)? How can faith in God's promises quench them?
3. How does walking in community with other believers strengthen your faith and protection compared to fighting alone?
4. What practical steps can you take this week to carry the gospel of peace to someone else?

After Action Review and Mission Orders

1. What went right? Did you stand firm in peace this week when anxiety tried to shake you? Did you raise the shield when temptation struck?
2. What went wrong? Where did you slip or stumble because you weren't grounded in the gospel? Where did you face arrows alone instead of linking shields with others?
3. How do we improve? Anchor yourself deeper in God's peace through prayer and Scripture. Practice raising the shield daily by recalling His promises. Link arms with brothers so your shield wall grows stronger.
4. Mission Orders: This week, put on your shoes of readiness

every morning and raise your shield of faith every time the enemy attacks. Stand firm. Advance with confidence. Lock arms with your brothers.

Remember: The ground may shake, the arrows may fly, but with peace and faith, you will not fall.

Chapter 14: The Armor of God - The Helmet and Sword

Paul next describes for us the helmet of salvation (Ephesians 6:17). For a Roman soldier, the helmet (galea) was not optional, and it most certainly wasn't just ceremonial. Made of bronze or iron, lined with leather for comfort, it often had cheek guards and a back plate to protect the neck. A single blow to the head could end the fight instantly, so the helmet was essential for survival.

Spiritually, salvation is our helmet. It guards the mind, the battlefield where most of the enemy's attacks begin. Doubt, fear, condemnation, lies, these are all strikes aimed at your head. The helmet reminds us that salvation is secure and that we are forgiven, adopted, redeemed, and sealed in Christ (Ephesians 1:13–14).

Without this helmet, a believer is vulnerable to crippling uncertainty. But when you put it on, you can withstand the blows of accusation and despair. Paul echoes this in 1 Thessalonians 5:8: *"But since we belong to the day, let us be sober, putting on faith and love as a breastplate, and the hope of salvation as a helmet."* Take notice that it is hope that protects your head.

When World War I began, soldiers often wore soft cloth or leather caps, which provided almost no protection from shrapnel, debris, or glancing bullets. The result of this was about 25% of fatalities were from head injuries. With the introduction of steel helmets though, casualty rates from head wounds dropped by close to 80%! A simple piece of armor drastically reduced battlefield deaths and similarly, many Christians fall because they don't "wear" the assurance of their salvation. But when our minds are covered with the hope of Christ, we can endure the shelling of the enemy.

Paul's description of the Sword of the Spirit in Ephesians 6:17 is intentional and strategic. Out of the entire list of the armor of God, it is the only offensive weapon given to us, and Paul makes it clear that this "sword" he is referring to is the Word of God. Roman soldiers of Paul's day were issued a gladius, a short, double-edged sword designed for precision strikes in close combat. It wasn't meant for wild, reckless swings, it was meant for controlled, intentional thrusts against the enemy.

And yet, many Christians today treat the Word like a bludgeon rather than a blade. Instead of training to wield Scripture with accuracy, they swing wildly, critiquing others, calling out sins publicly, and weaponizing the Bible to shame rather than restore. But that was never God's intention. The Sword of the Spirit was never designed to attack fellow soldiers in the Kingdom; it was given so we can stand firm against the real enemy (Ephesians 6:12). When we spend more time fighting each other than fighting Satan, we're actually leaving ourselves defenseless where it matters most.

Paul's point is clear, the sword isn't about volume; it's about precision. It's not about being loud, brash, and offensive for the sake of being right, it's about piercing lies with truth and defeating darkness with the light of God's Word. The enemy loves when we turn the sword on one another, because while we're busy cutting down our brothers, he advances his position unopposed.

The Word of God is sharper than any two-edged sword (Hebrews 4:12). It penetrates hearts, exposes lies, and cuts through deception. But notice, the Word only works if we know it and use it. A sword still in its sheath is no help in a fight. Jesus Himself modeled this in Matthew 4 when Satan tempted Him in the wilderness. Each time, Jesus responded not with opinions or emotions, but with Scripture: *"It is written."*

The Spirit empowers the Word to cut precisely where needed. In the hands of a trained believer, Scripture deflects temptation, dismantles lies, and pierces hearts with truth.

There was a season, not as long ago as I would like, where my thoughts were constantly under attack with doubts about God's love, lies about my worth, and anxiety about my situation. It felt like a barrage to the head every day. Ultimately, what saved me was the helmet of salvation, reminding myself daily, "I am saved, I am secure, I am His."

During that time though, I also learned to wield the sword. I stopped just reading Scripture passively and started speaking it, praying it, and declaring it out loud. The more I did, the more the lies lost their power. The Word wasn't just information...it became my weapon.

Drills and Practice

1. Helmet Drill: Each morning, declare your salvation out loud. Example: "I am a child of God. I am saved, forgiven, and sealed in Christ." Let this be the helmet you put on before the day begins.
2. Sword Drill: Choose three verses that address the enemy's common attacks against you (fear, temptation, shame). Memorize them and practice speaking them out loud when those attacks come.
3. Combat Training: Read through Matthew 4:1–11 and note how Jesus used Scripture in battle. Write your own "It is written" responses to situations you regularly face.

Thoughts & Discussion Questions

1. Why is assurance of salvation critical for guarding the mind? How do you "wear" the helmet daily?
2. When was the last time you felt the enemy's blows against your thoughts? How did you respond?
3. How comfortable are you with wielding the Word as a weapon? Do you tend to leave your sword sheathed, or do you actively use it?

4. What steps can you take to grow in Scripture memorization and application so that the Word becomes second nature in battle?

After Action Review and Mission Orders

1. What went right? Did you remind yourself of your salvation and stand firm in hope this week? Did you unsheathe the Word in moments of temptation?
2. What went wrong? Where did you allow doubt or lies to strike your mind because your helmet wasn't secure? Did you leave your sword hanging when the battle raged?
3. How do we improve? Strengthen your assurance through daily reminders of the gospel. Sharpen your sword through memorization, prayer, and application. Practice saying "It is written" until it becomes instinct.
4. Mission Orders: This week, guard your thoughts with the helmet of salvation and go on the offensive with the sword of the Spirit. Do not settle for defense alone, advance by speaking God's truth into every situation.

Remember: Stand strong, strike true, and remember: the victory is already yours in Christ.

Chapter 15: The Warrior's Weapon - Prayer

If the armor equips and protects us and the sword enables us to fight, then prayer is the lifeline that keeps us connected to the Commander Himself. Paul closes the Armor of God passage with this command: *"And pray in the Spirit on all occasions with all kinds of prayers and requests. With this in mind, be alert and always keep on praying for all the Lord's people"* (Ephesians 6:18).

Prayer is not an optional afterthought. It is the battlefield radio, the signal flare, the direct line to headquarters. Without prayer, we are soldiers cut off from command, trying to guess the strategy and survive on our own. With prayer, we are in constant contact with our King, receiving orders, strength, and reinforcements.

Too many men view prayer as a polite habit before meals or bedtime, or as an emergency flare when things get bad. But prayer is so much more, it is a weapon that calls heaven's power into earthly battles.

James 5:16 tells us plainly: *"The prayer of a righteous person is powerful and effective."* That word "effective" in the original Greek means energized, active, dynamic. Prayer is not passive; it accomplishes real movement in the spiritual realm.

Paul uses military urgency when he says to pray "on all occasions." That means before the fight, during the fight, and after the fight. We do not lower our guard after a single prayer; we stay in the flow of communication with God.

It's hard to believe in our current society, but prayer was an actual tool in the arsenal of our governments not that many years ago. In World War II, General Dwight Eisenhower prepared his men for the now famous D-Day invasion. But beyond the troops, tanks, and planes, there was another force at work: prayer. Across the Allied nations, churches gathered by the thousands to intercede. In Britain, King George VI even called for a National Day of Prayer before the invasion.

When the stormy weather threatened to cancel the landings, Eisenhower wrestled with the decision. At the eleventh hour, the weather unexpectedly cleared, opening a narrow window that allowed the invasion to proceed. Many historians still call it "a miracle of timing." Soldiers carried weapons and rations, but it was prayer that moved the hand of God to open the way for victory.

Prayer doesn't always change the circumstances instantly, but it always changes the battle. It brings divine intervention where human strength runs out.

It was fairly recently that I experienced a season of ministry where I felt like I was under constant fire. The weight of responsibility, criticism, and spiritual attacks were so heavy that I wondered if I could, or should, keep going. I had put on my armor, but I was still weary. I was drained, worn out, and frustrated.

It was during a late-night men's meeting with a small group of brothers that I felt a breakthrough. Although I was leading the meeting, I had brothers who recognized I was struggling and reached out with their support. As they laid hands on me and prayed in the Spirit, it was like reinforcements arrived. Strength returned. Peace filled me. The battle didn't stop, but I was no longer fighting alone. In that moment, prayer called in God's power and reminded me that the Commander was still on the field with me.

Drills and Practice

1. Prayer Watch: Set alarms at three different points in your day. Each time, stop what you're doing, even if for 60 seconds, and pray specifically for strength, clarity, and protection. This keeps you "always alert."
2. Target Practice: Write down the names of three men who are in the fight with you. Pray for them daily this week, by name,

with specific requests.

3. Battlefield Report: Each evening, journal one prayer God answered that day, even if small. This trains you to see how He is active in the fight.

Thoughts & Discussion Questions

1. Do you see prayer more as a ritual or a weapon? How can this perspective shift?
2. When have you experienced prayer changing the "weather" in your life, turning the tide in ways you couldn't explain?
3. What distractions or obstacles keep you from maintaining constant communication with God?
4. How can your small group or brotherhood strengthen one another through prayer?

After Action Review and Mission Orders

1. What went right? Did you maintain open communication with God this week, or did you cut the line until a crisis hit? Did you lift up brothers in prayer by name?
2. What went wrong? Where did you neglect prayer, treating it as an afterthought instead of a weapon?
3. How do we improve? Build habits of consistent prayer. Train yourself to pray quickly and often, not just long and formal. Lean on the Spirit to guide you when words fail.
4. Mission Orders: This week, commit to wielding prayer as your weapon. Call down God's power before you walk into meetings, temptations, conflicts, and opportunities.

Remember: Don't fight disconnected, stay on the line with the Commander. A warrior cut off from command is vulnerable, but a warrior in constant contact is unstoppable.

Chapter 16: The Power of Brotherhood

The world loves the myth of the lone warrior. We glorify men who stand alone, bleeding, bruised, and unbroken, taking on impossible odds with nothing but sheer grit and a loaded magazine. We make heroes out of Rambo tearing through the jungle, Jack Reacher walking into town with nothing but a toothbrush and leaving a trail of wreckage behind him, John Wick avenging his dog with an army's worth of ammo, and Maximus in Gladiator standing defiant before the emperor.

These men are tough, relentless, and unstoppable...or so it seems. Culture tells us real strength means needing no one. It whispers that depending on others is weakness, that brotherhood is optional, and that if you're really "a man," you'll figure it out alone.

But here's the truth: in the real world, lone warriors die first. Armies don't win wars because of one unstoppable man, they win because of trained, unified, disciplined brotherhood. Every soldier knows the first rule of survival: watch your six, and someone watches yours. If you're alone on the battlefield, you're a target.

And spiritually, the stakes are even higher. The enemy would love nothing more than to isolate you, cut you off from your brothers, and leave you fighting alone. That's where men fall. That's where marriages crumble. That's where faith collapses.

That image of the lone warrior that our culture loves, the man with grit, determination, and no need for anyone else. Hollywood paints him as the hero who single-handedly takes down the enemy. But Scripture tells a very different story.

From the very beginning, God declared, *"It is not good for man to be alone"* (Genesis 2:18). That statement was not just about marriage, it was about the human condition. God designed us for connection. Isolation is not strength; it is weakness disguised as independence.

Ecclesiastes 4:9–10 puts it plainly, *"Two are better than one, because they have a good return for their labor: If either of them falls down, one can help the other up. But pity anyone who falls and has no one to help them up."* The enemy knows this truth, which is why one of his favorite tactics is to separate men from their brothers.

Satan is no fool. He has studied human nature for millennia and he knows that men are most vulnerable when isolated. Just as lions hunt by separating a weak animal from the herd, the enemy prowls around looking for the lone soldier who has stepped away from his band of brothers (1 Peter 5:8).

Think about it, when do most men fall into temptation, despair, or defeat? It's when they're alone. How often are you sitting with a group of friends and pull out your phone to queue up a great porn video? Have you recently been sitting with friends at a friendly get together when you decided to break out your lines of cocaine because life is just tough? Pornography, addiction, secret sin, depression, discouragement...these often flourish in the soil of isolation.

Brotherhood isn't just about friendship; it's about survival.

I'm sure you have heard of the Battle of the Bulge that happened in December 1944. It was here that the 101st Airborne Division was surrounded in Bastogne, Belgium. Their supplies were critically low, the temperatures were brutal, and the Germans demanded surrender. But the men of Easy Company stood together.

When General McAuliffe famously responded "Nuts!" to the German surrender demand, it wasn't bravado, it was brotherhood. Those men endured hunger, frostbite, and relentless attacks, but because they fought side by side, they held their ground until reinforcements arrived. The lesson is clear: men who fight together can withstand what no man could survive alone.

The men of Easy Company understood something that too many Christian men today have forgotten: victory requires brotherhood. They weren't stronger because they had better weapons, more supplies, or superior numbers, they were stronger because they refused to fight alone. When one foxhole came under fire, another covered them. When a man was wounded, his brothers dragged him to safety. When one lost heart, another spoke courage back into him.

This is the picture of spiritual warfare that we discussed in the previous chapters when Paul calls us to *"put on the full armor of God."* Armor isn't designed for a man fighting solo, it's designed for men advancing together. As I explained earlier, Roman soldiers locked their shields in a formation called the testudo, or tortoise. Alone, a soldier was vulnerable; together, they were nearly untouchable. Paul knew that when he wrote to the church in Ephesus. The church was never meant to be a collection of isolated warriors; it was built to be an unbreakable line of brothers standing shoulder to shoulder.

Hebrews 10:24–25 reminds us, *"And let us consider how we may spur one another on toward love and good deeds, not giving up meeting together, as some are in the habit of doing, but encouraging one another—and all the more as you see the Day approaching."* Encouragement isn't a suggestion. Brotherhood isn't optional. It's a command straight from Scripture. And yet, too many men buy into the lie that they can handle it on their own. We drift from our brothers, stop showing up to men's groups, pull back from accountability, and before we know it, we're isolated, which is exactly where the enemy wants us.

The truth is simple, you will not win this fight alone. You can't carry your marriage, your faith, your calling, and your struggles on your own shoulders. God designed you to walk with brothers who sharpen you (Proverbs 27:17), restore you when you stumble (Galatians 6:1), and stand guard over your six when the arrows of the enemy start flying.

The men of the 101st stood because they stood together. You and I are called to do the same.

Drills and Practice

1. Battle Buddy: Choose one man this week and commit to praying for him daily. Text or call him midweek to check on his fight.
2. Foxhole Check: Make a list of the men who truly know your struggles. If the list is empty, your foxhole is empty. Start filling it.
3. Shoulder to Shoulder: Meet face-to-face with one brother this week, not just surface talk, but honest conversation about battles and victories.

Thoughts & Discussion Questions

1. Why do men often resist brotherhood, preferring to go it alone?
2. How has isolation made you vulnerable in the past?
3. Who are the brothers you can count on in the fight? Are you being that kind of brother to someone else?
4. What steps can your group take to become more than acquaintances—true warriors together?

After Action Review and Mission Orders

1. What went right? Did you stand with your brothers this week? Did you lift someone when they fell?
2. What went wrong? Where did you isolate, hide, or refuse to ask for help?
3. How do we improve? Build habits of brotherhood. Don't wait for crisis, forge connections now.
4. Mission Orders: This week, refuse to fight alone. Identify your battle buddy, check on your brothers, and let them into your fight.

Remember: One man standing alone may be taken down, but two standing back-to-back can resist, and a cord of three strands is not quickly broken (Ecclesiastes 4:12).

Chapter 17: The Warrior's Training vs. Battleground

The battlefield doesn't care how loud you roar.

It doesn't care how tough you look, how many motivational quotes you've posted, or how many sermons you've heard. When the first shots are fired, when chaos erupts around you, and when fear claws at your throat, there is only one question that matters: Did you train for this, or not?

Every warrior knows the difference between the training ground and the battleground. Training is where you sweat so you don't bleed. Training is where your discipline is forged, your instincts sharpened, and your body pushed beyond what your mind thinks it can endure. The battleground is something entirely different. It's not controlled. It's not comfortable. And it sure isn't forgiving. On the battleground, hesitation costs lives.

But here's the problem: too many Christian men treat life's battleground like it's practice. They improvise. They wing it. They hope that when temptation blindsides them, when their marriage hits the rocks, when their faith gets tested in the fire, they'll somehow "rise to the occasion."

Brother, listen to me—you never rise to the occasion.

You fall to the level of your training. Every. Single. Time.

Ask any Navy SEAL who's been under fire. Ask any Roman legionary who faced a wall of screaming Gauls. Ask the paratroopers of the 101st Airborne who dropped into Normandy on D-Day. When the world was exploding around them, when plans fell apart, when chaos reigned, their survival didn't depend on improvisation. It depended on what had been drilled into them until it became muscle memory.

And yet, in the church today, too many men step into spiritual combat completely unprepared. We spend more time scrolling

Instagram than sharpening the Sword of the Spirit. We binge Netflix but can't quote a single verse when the enemy attacks. We hit the gym to build bigger arms but let our prayer life atrophy. Then we wonder why we're losing ground in our marriages, our homes, and our faith.

Satan doesn't wait for you to get ready. He doesn't pause the fight so you can catch up on your quiet time. When the attack comes, and it will come, the time for preparation is over.

Training time is right now.

This chapter isn't about playing church. It's about getting battle-ready. We're going to break down what it means to prepare like a warrior of God, how to discipline your mind, heart, and habits, and how to fight with skill instead of panic. Because the truth is simple: if you don't train, you will be taken out.

The question is, are you preparing like your life, your family, and your faith depend on it? Because they do.

Paul told Timothy, *"Train yourself for godliness"* (1 Timothy 4:7). Notice the critical word in that passage...TRAIN. Godliness doesn't happen by accident. It takes intentional practice. Soldiers drill daily not because they love repetition, but because repetition produces readiness.

You may have seen the Hollywood movie about it, but on October 3, 1993 in Mogadishu, Somalia, the mission was supposed to be simple and take all of about 30 minutes. In and out. But within minutes, everything collapsed into chaos. Two Black Hawks were down, convoys were lost, and hundreds of U.S. Army Rangers and Delta Force operators suddenly found themselves trapped in a hostile city of thousands.

In the deafening roar of gunfire and RPG explosions, soldiers were forced to make split-second decisions under unimaginable pressure. Streets turned into ambush zones. Humvees got shredded. Entire squads were separated and pinned down. For many, the difference between life and death came down to one thing: training.

There was no time to stop and debate tactics. No time to check manuals. No chance to "figure it out" on the fly. Soldiers who had drilled movement under fire, close-quarters combat, and casualty evacuation didn't have to think, they simply reacted. Muscle memory took over. They cleared rooms, returned fire, and dragged wounded brothers to cover without hesitation because they had rehearsed those motions hundreds of times before.

But for those who hadn't trained as rigorously, hesitation cost lives. In Mogadishu, the battlefield punished indecision. Improvisation without preparation was deadly.

That's the brutal truth, you don't rise to the occasion...you fall to the level of your training.

And spiritually, the stakes are even higher. Life will hit you with ambushes you never see coming: a sudden loss, a temptation that blindsides you, a crisis in your marriage, an attack on your faith. In those moments, you don't have time to "figure it out," you will fight the way you've trained.

Mogadishu proved that discipline, repetition, and preparation are what greatly increases the odds to keep warriors alive in the chaos. In the same way, prayer, Scripture, accountability, and brotherhood prepare you for the spiritual firefight you will face. The battlefield is no place to improvise.

Training for the Christian warrior means spiritual disciplines. Just like pushups build chest and arms, disciplines build spiritual strength:

- Prayer – Not just in crisis, but daily, steady conversation with the Commander-in-Chief.
- Scripture – Reading, studying, memorizing, and meditating on the Word, sharpening the sword daily.
- Fasting – Training the body to submit so the spirit can lead.
- Fellowship – Consistent connection with brothers who sharpen and challenge.

- Obedience in Small Things – Faithfulness in the daily "drills" makes you trustworthy in the big battles.

Without training, the armor feels heavy, the sword feels clumsy, and the fight feels impossible. But with training, the armor becomes natural, the sword becomes sharp, and the fight becomes purposeful.

Still not sure that all the training is worth it? Consider this...in 480 BC, the world watched one of history's most legendary last stands unfold. At the narrow pass of Thermopylae, 300 Spartan warriors stood shoulder-to-shoulder against the colossal might of the Persian Empire. King Xerxes had assembled one of the largest armies the ancient world had ever seen, estimated to be over 250,000 soldiers, while the Greeks defending the pass numbered barely 7,000 in total, with the Spartans forming the razor's edge of the spear.

By every natural measure, the Spartans were doomed. Yet for three brutal days, they held their ground. Wave after wave of Persian soldiers crashed against their shields like a tidal surge, but the line never broke. Why? Training.

From the time a Spartan boy was seven years old, he was taken from his family and enrolled in the agōgē, a ruthless military training program designed to forge warriors capable of standing when others fled. They were drilled daily in weapons, tactics, and endurance. They were taught to fight as a unit, shields locked, spears thrusting as one, moving like a single body under the command of their king. Pain wasn't avoided; it was embraced. Hunger, exhaustion, and suffering were not accidents of life but essential parts of their preparation.

This was why 300 men could stand against hundreds of thousands. When the arrows darkened the sky, they didn't panic, they tightened the line. When exhaustion set in, they didn't crumble, their bodies responded out of muscle memory. They had already faced death a thousand times in training, so on the battlefield, they didn't improvise... they executed.

And that's the principle we must not miss here, victory isn't won in the moment of battle; it's won in the years of preparation before the battle ever comes.

Spiritually, the same truth applies. We are at war, it may not be with flesh and blood but rather against the rulers, powers, and forces of darkness (Ephesians 6:12). The enemy's forces are vast, relentless, and well-organized. But victory doesn't come from being louder, braver, or stronger in the moment. It comes from relentless training in God's Word, prayer, accountability, and spiritual discipline.

You will not rise to the occasion when temptation hits, when the diagnosis comes, when the marriage crisis explodes, or when doubt attacks your faith. You will fall to the level of your training.

The Spartans didn't stand because they were fearless, they stood because they were prepared. But heads up...God calls us to prepare the same way.

Drills and Practice

1. Bible Drill: Choose one verse each week to memorize. Say it daily, write it out, and quote it in prayer.
2. Prayer Rhythm: Set three times a day (morning, midday, night) for intentional prayer. Even five minutes of focused prayer sharpens readiness.
3. Fasting Practice: Fast one meal a week, using that time to pray for victory over a specific battle.
4. Brotherhood Training: Once a week, share with your brother one thing God taught you in your training. Iron sharpens iron (Proverbs 27:17).

Thoughts & Discussion Questions

1. How have you seen the difference between being spiritually "in shape" vs. out of shape?
2. What discipline do you find most difficult to maintain and

why?
3. How does training in private prepare you for battles in public?
4. Who can you invite into your training to hold you accountable?

After Action Review and Mission Orders

1. What went right? Did you practice consistent discipline this week? Did training sharpen your response in real situations?
2. What went wrong? Where did laziness or inconsistency creep in?
3. How do we improve? Establish daily rhythms and guardrails. Don't wait until battle—train now.
4. Mission Orders: This week, build your training plan. Pick one discipline to strengthen, one verse to memorize, and one brother to share your progress with.

Remember: Discipline today is victory tomorrow.

Chapter 18: The Warrior's Resolve – Perseverance in Suffering

Every warrior who steps onto the battlefield knows one thing with absolute certainty: pain is coming. We have trained for months, sharpen our swords, memorized the plan, and studied every map, but the moment the first round cracks overhead or the first blade clashes, all illusions of comfort vanish. The battlefield is chaos. It's loud, it's bloody, and it's unforgiving. Soldiers aren't surprised by pain; we expect it. We know wounds will come and we know exhaustion will set in. We know that fear will stalk us like a shadow.

The Christian life is no different.

Somewhere along the way, modern Western Christianity started selling a soft gospel that promises ease, comfort, and blessing without cost. But that's not what Scripture teaches. Paul doesn't sugarcoat it for us. He tells us straight, *"Indeed, all who desire to live a godly life in Christ Jesus will be persecuted"* (2 Timothy 3:12).

Not might...Will. Not maybe...Definitely. Not sometimes...Always. Suffering is a probability, it's a guarantee.

"In this world you will have trouble. But take heart! I have overcome the world" (John 16:33). Trouble isn't a possibility, it's a guarantee. Suffering isn't an exception, it's the expectation. The question isn't if the blows will come; the question is whether you'll still be standing when they do.

Because make no mistake, the enemy wants you broken, bleeding, and believing the lie that you're alone. He wants your faith fractured, your hope drained, your resolve shattered. He wants you so worn down by hardship that surrender feels easier than obedience.

But warriors don't break...They endure.

And endurance doesn't happen by accident...It's forged. It's hammered out in the fire of preparation long before the battle ever starts. Ask any soldier who's faced real combat, you don't rise to the occasion when bullets start flying... you fall to the level of your training. That's why this chapter matters, because whether you realize it or not, you are in a war. And the suffering you're walking through right now isn't meaningless, it's shaping you. The pain is forging something eternal. You're not just fighting to survive; you're training to overcome.

Let's look at some suffering that happened in Korea in December 1950. The temperature was 40 degrees below zero, and the wind howled like a living thing, slicing through every layer of clothing. Frostbite claimed fingers and toes faster than bullets could, and rifles jammed solid with ice. Over 30,000 U.S. Marines of the 1st Marine Division were surrounded by nearly 120,000 Chinese soldiers at the Chosin Reservoir. The were outnumbered almost 4 to 1.

The order came down: "Retreat." But Marines don't retreat, they attack in a different direction.

For two weeks, the men clawed their way through mountains, waist-deep snow, and relentless ambushes. Every night, the wounded froze where they fell. Yet, somehow, the line never broke.

Why? Because training had prepared them for this. Discipline replaced despair. Small units moved as one, executing maneuvers they had drilled until they became muscle memory. When interviewed later, survivors repeated the same mantra, "We were Marines. We had a job to do. Quitting was never an option."

Against overwhelming odds, they fought their way 78 miles to the sea, bringing their dead, their wounded, and their honor with them. Historians call it a "strategic withdrawal," but the Marines call it the day resolve beat suffering.

This Battle of Chosin Reservoir is a stark reminder for us as Christian warriors, you don't get to choose the terrain, the weather, or the enemy's numbers. What you do choose is your resolve.

Paul told Timothy, *"Endure hardship as a good soldier of Christ Jesus"* (2 Timothy 2:3).

When the fight gets cold, when the odds seem impossible, and when the enemy surrounds you, you don't survive by improvising, you endure because you've been trained. Your spiritual drills of prayer, Scripture, brotherhood, and worship are the difference between folding under pressure and fighting through to victory. Like the Marines at Chosin, you may be outnumbered, but you are not outmatched when your training has forged your resolve.

To persevere means to remain, to endure, and to keep standing when everything in us wants to quit. It is grit baptized in faith. Hebrews 10:36 says, *"You need perseverance so that when you have done the will of God, you will receive what He has promised."* Perseverance is not passive. It is an active decision you must make to keep fighting, keep praying, keep believing, even when tears blur your vision and wounds slow your pace.

I have had the honor of spending many hours talking with World War II veterans and each and every time I find myself in awe of the heroism those men and women demonstrated. During their war, thousands of Allied soldiers were captured and thrown into some of the most brutal prison camps in human history. These weren't simply holding cells, they were hell on earth. Prisoners were crammed into bamboo cages so small they couldn't stand upright. Disease ran rampant with dysentery, malaria, and cholera claimed lives daily. The meager rations barely kept men alive with only being given handfuls of rice, sometimes crawling with maggots, paired with dirty water that spread sickness more than it quenched thirst.

Beatings were constant and unpredictable with the guards punishing men for collapsing under exhaustion, for failing to work fast enough, or simply because cruelty became their sport. They were forced into back-breaking slave labor of laying railroad tracks with bleeding hands, carrying heavy logs barefoot over sharp stones, digging graves for the friends who had died beside them the night before. Winter brought biting frost that split skin to the bone, while summer turned camps into sweltering ovens swarming with insects and rot.

And yet, some men survived. These survivors had strong minds and unbreakable spirits and they testified that the will to endure was forged in hope. It was the resolve to believe there was something worth living for in their family, freedom, faith, or brotherhood. That quiet, relentless determination became their lifeline. It was their shield when their bodies had nothing left to give.

In the same way, spiritual perseverance keeps us alive in enemy territory. Without it, despair consumes us. While with it, hope sustains us.

Perseverance brings to mind the Bataan Death March, but you need to understand this wasn't just a march as the name implies, it was a slow, brutal exodus through hell. In April 1942, after the fall of Bataan, approximately 76,000 American and Filipino soldiers surrendered to the Japanese. What followed though was a 65-mile forced march through scorching heat, dense jungle, and unrelenting cruelty. Prisoners, already weakened by disease, hunger, and dehydration, were crushed into wooden formations and beaten mercilessly by guards. The sun was their enemy so intense that POWs were forced to strip in the blazing heat, exposed with no shade or water, while those near them fell and fried on the roadside.

If a man collapsed, he didn't get help, he got a bayonet. There were no mercy patrols. One survivor described how truck-mounted "cleanup crews" ran over fallen soldiers on purpose, ensuring they couldn't resist any longer while others were beheaded. At the Pantingan River, around 400 Filipino and American officers were bound, lined up, and slaughtered in cold blood by their captors.

Survivor Lester Tenney, a tank commander captured early in the Battle of Bataan, recalled the horror: "It wasn't a march. It was a trudge," he said. They marched for ten days with no food or water, collapsing one by one. Those too weak to go on were killed instantly, two seconds was all it took.

Those who survived to make it to Camp O'Donnell faced another nightmare. The camp was never designed for such numbers as it was built for 10,000 yet holding 70,000. Prisoners lived in cramped bamboo huts, without blankets, plumbing, or clean water. Malaria, dysentery, beri-beri, and starvation claimed thousands more lives every day. Survivors were forced into mass graves behind barbed-wire fences just to bury their dead. Some camps saw hundreds of deaths per day.

This brutal march shows us what real endurance looks like in physical, mental, and spiritual resilience while in the midst of concentrated suffering. These men didn't survive because of their strength, they survived because something inside them refused to die: hope, faith in something bigger than themselves, bond with brothers, and unshakable resolve.

I've walked through seasons of deep discouragement, although nothing even close to what those World War II veterans endured. I've had times when ministry felt empty, when relationships fractured, when the weight of failure pressed like a crushing burden. I've stumbled through compromise and carried shame heavier than any pack. But every time I thought about quitting, God's Spirit whispered: "Get up. Keep moving. The fight isn't over."

Looking back, the greatest growth in my faith hasn't come during times of comfort but during times of pain. Suffering has been both my fire and my forge. My resolve was not built in easy days, but in the nights I wept on my knees and chose, by faith, to trust God anyway.

Why Perseverance Matters

1. It proves our faith genuine: 1 Peter 1:7 says trials test and refine our faith like gold. Perseverance shows that our trust is more than words.
2. It strengthens our character: Romans 5:3–4 reminds us that

suffering produces perseverance; perseverance, character; and character, hope.

3. It glorifies God: When others see us endure suffering with faith, it testifies to God's power, not our own.
4. It prepares us for reward: James 1:12 promises, "Blessed is the man who remains steadfast under trial, for when he has stood the test he will receive the crown of life."

Drills and Practice

1. Resolve Journal: Each day, write one sentence declaring your choice to persevere. Example: "Today I choose to endure in faith, no matter what comes."
2. Endurance Prayer: Set aside 10 minutes daily to pray specifically for strength in suffering. Name your battles and ask God to fortify your resolve.
3. Witness in Suffering: Share with one brother where you are tempted to quit. Ask him to remind you of truth when you waver.
4. Physical Training Parallel: Push your body in one exercise past the point of comfort. Let the discipline of physical perseverance remind you that spiritual perseverance works the same way.

Thoughts & Discussion Questions

1. Where in your life right now do you feel the weight of suffering or discouragement most heavily?
2. Have you ever seen God use suffering to build strength in you? How?
3. What are the practical ways you can "take heart" (John 16:33) in the middle of trials?
4. Who can you lean on when your strength feels gone?

After Action Review and Mission Orders

1. What went right? Did you endure a trial this week by holding to God's promises?
2. What went wrong? Did you let discouragement turn into despair? Did you isolate instead of reaching out?
3. How do we improve? Anchor deeper into God's Word, lean on brothers, and remind yourself of the eternal reward.
4. Mission Orders: This week, identify one area where you are tempted to quit. Write down three Scriptures that directly speak to perseverance (Romans 5:3–5, James 1:12, Hebrews 12:1–3). Memorize them. When the enemy whispers "give up," declare God's Word out loud.

Remember: The warrior's greatest weapon is not comfort but resolve.

Chapter 19: The Warrior's Victory – Standing Firm Until the End

The battlefield is littered with the fallen, men who started strong but couldn't endure the fight. They charged in with passion, weapons blazing, but somewhere along the way, fatigue set in. Fear crept close. Compromise whispered sweet lies. And little by little, they lowered their guard...until the enemy claimed them.

Every warrior knows the sobering truth that it's not enough to start the fight, you have to finish it. The Christian life is not a sprint, it's a lifelong war. Battles will rage across seasons, some quick and violent, others slow and grinding. And while many prepare for the opening clash, few prepare for the grind that follows. But Jesus was clear: *"But the one who endures to the end will be saved."* (Matthew 24:13)

This isn't about earning salvation by sheer grit, it's about proving the reality of your faith by lasting when others walk away. Real warriors don't quit when the fight gets bloody, instead they plant their feet, square their shoulders, and refuse to surrender.

Just look at history: wars aren't won by the strongest army in the first hour, they're won by the army that refuses to break in the final one. And make no mistake, brother, the enemy is betting on your surrender. He's counting on wearing you down, convincing you it's easier to compromise, quit, or coast to the finish line. But you weren't called to coast, you were called to conquer.

Victory doesn't belong to the fastest, the loudest, or even the strongest, it belongs to the one who still stands when the smoke clears. So the question isn't how strong you started, the question isw ill you still be standing when it's over?

Victory in the kingdom of God is not defined the same way the world defines it. The world says victory is comfort, wealth, applause, or recognition, but God says victory is faithfulness. Victory is keeping your eyes fixed on Jesus, even when the crowd boos, even when you're bruised and bloodied. Victory is crossing the finish line with scars but still standing in Christ.

Paul captured it best in 2 Timothy 4:7–8, *"I have fought the good fight, I have finished the race, I have kept the faith. Now there is in store for me the crown of righteousness, which the Lord, the righteous Judge, will award to me on that day—and not only to me, but also to all who have longed for His appearing."* That's victory...not perfection...not applause...but finishing still clinging to Christ.

Consider during the Tet Offensive in January 1968 when U.S. Marines were ordered into Hue City, Vietnam. What they walked into was an absolute nightmare. The enemy had seized control of the city, fortified every street, and turned homes, shops, and even churches into kill zones. For nearly a month, the Marines fought house to house, room by room in close-quarters urban combat where every corner could hide death. There were no front lines but instead danger came from every direction.

The conditions were brutal. Supplies were scarce. Ammunition sometimes ran low. Sleep was a luxury no one could afford. Rain poured constantly, soaking uniforms, rusting weapons, and chilling men to the bone. The stench of smoke, blood, and decay filled the air. And yet, they pressed forward.

Every day they gained inches, not miles. Every doorway cleared came with a cost in friends wounded and brothers killed. But despite overwhelming fatigue, despite heavy losses, despite the temptation to pull back, they refused to retreat.

After weeks of relentless fighting, the Marines retook Hue. It was one of the bloodiest battles of the Vietnam War, but their unyielding resolve turned what looked like certain defeat into victory.

That is exactly what it means to stand firm until the end. Victory doesn't come from comfort, ease, or shortcuts. It comes from warriors who refuse to break when the battle grinds on longer than expected.

The parallel is striking: victory isn't always escape from suffering, but faithfulness in the face of impossible odds. The Christian warrior's Hue City is daily life, standing firm in Christ when everything in culture pushes you to bow.

Standing firm doesn't always mean moving forward at full speed, sometimes it simply means not retreating. There have been days when my victory was simply refusing to quit. And often, that "refusal" became the seed of breakthrough.

But why does standing firm matter so much?

1. It honors Christ: We stand because He stood for us, carrying the cross to the very end.
2. It inspires others: Your endurance strengthens the brotherhood. Courage is contagious.
3. It defeats the enemy's lies: Satan's greatest weapon is discouragement. Refusing to quit breaks his hold.
4. It secures eternal reward: Revelation 2:10, "Be faithful unto death, and I will give you the crown of life."

Drills and Practice

1. Victory Verse Memorization: Commit 2 Timothy 4:7–8 to memory. Declare it daily.
2. Stand Firm Exercise: Choose one area of your life where compromise tempts you. Make a written commitment: "Here I will not yield." Share it with a brother.
3. Battle Cry: Each morning, pray: "Lord, today I will stand in Your strength. Even if I fall, I will rise again in Your power."
4. Physical Parallel: Hold a plank position or a wall sit longer than you think you can. Train your body to endure, reminding yourself that spiritual endurance is the greater fight.

Thoughts & Discussion Questions

1. What does "victory" look like to you...and does it match God's definition?
2. Where in your life are you tempted to lay down your sword too early?
3. How does your endurance, or lack of it, affect the men around you?
4. How does the hope of eternal reward strengthen you in daily battles?

After Action Review and Mission Orders

1. What went right? Did you resist the enemy's push to quit this week? Did you stand firm in a moment of temptation?
2. What went wrong? Did you retreat into compromise or silence when you should have stood in truth?
3. How do we improve? Build your resolve in God's promises, lean on the brotherhood, and remember the eternal reward that cannot be shaken.
4. Mission Orders: This week, stand firm in one area where the enemy has consistently attacked. Use Scripture as your shield, prayer as your weapon, and brotherhood as your backup. Refuse to yield.

Remember: Your orders are simple: don't quit. Don't bow. Don't retreat. Stand firm. Victory belongs to those who finish in Christ.

Chapter 20: The Warrior's Legacy – Passing the Torch

Every warrior eventually lays down his weapon. Every fighter eventually hears the bell for the final round. You and I will not live forever on this battlefield and one day, your heart will beat its last, and your war will end.

But before that day comes, you need to answer a critical question: what happens after you? Because this fight is bigger than your story. It's bigger than your career, your comfort, or even your lifetime. The battle you're in right now is not just for your soul, it's for the souls that come after you.

Psalm 78:4–7 says it like this, *"We will not hide them from their children; we will tell the next generation the praiseworthy deeds of the Lord, His power, and the wonders He has done...so the next generation would know them, even the children yet to be born, and they in turn would tell their children. Then they would put their trust in God and would not forget His deeds but would keep His commands."*

This is legacy.

This is your true mission: to hand off the torch still burning, to pass the baton of faith still in motion, to raise up warriors who will take their place on the front lines long after you're gone.

History proves it, kingdoms fall when men stop training the next generation. Armies collapse when the veterans stop investing in the recruits. Entire movements die when warriors stop making disciples.

The enemy knows this, too. If he can't take you out, he'll go after your sons, your daughters, your brothers in Christ. He'll whisper, "Just focus on your fight. Just survive your battle." But you weren't called to just survive, you were called to multiply.

A real warrior lives with his eyes on eternity. He knows his scars, his victories, and even his failures are not wasted, instead they are a manual for the men coming behind him. Your endurance, your battles, your testimony...these are not just trophies on your shelf. They're tools in someone else's hands.

The question is, when you lay your weapon down, will anyone be strong enough to pick it up? In our world, legacy often means money, land, or a name etched in history books. But in God's kingdom, legacy means faith. A Godly legacy isn't measured in possessions but in disciples. It isn't what you leave for your children, but what you leave in your children.

Moses knew this. As Israel prepared to enter the Promised Land, Moses told the people in Deuteronomy 6:6–7, *"These commandments that I give you today are to be on your hearts. Impress them on your children. Talk about them when you sit at home and when you walk along the road, when you lie down and when you get up."*

The command was simple: pass the torch. Teach them. Model it. Talk about it in everyday life.

Consider the legacy demonstrated by General Dwight D. Eisenhower on the eve of D-Day as he walked among his men. The night was thick with uncertainty. Thousands of soldiers knew there was a good chance they might not return. Eisenhower didn't just give orders, he gave presence, encouragement, and a reminder of why they fought.

Later, historians would note that his presence in those fields gave courage to men who stormed the beaches the next day. Eisenhower was passing more than orders; he was passing strength, resolve, and purpose. That's legacy. It's not simply writing instructions; it's embodying them in a way that lives beyond you.

I think back to my own dad when I consider this. He didn't preach many sermons or normally stand in front of the church, but he has provided many lessons in how he has lived. His work ethic, his humor, his steady love for his family, these are all things that have shaped me. Even now, I carry phrases and habits I caught from him, not because he sat me down in a classroom, but because he modeled them day in and day out.

That's how faith is passed down. Your kids, your disciples, the young men around you, they don't just learn from what you say, they learn from how you stand. Your scars, your integrity, your consistency, that's your testimony, and it will either strengthen or weaken the generation after you.

Faith is fragile if not passed down and in fact, Judges 2:10 says, *"After that whole generation had been gathered to their ancestors, another generation grew up who neither knew the Lord nor what He had done for Israel."* One missed handoff can lead to spiritual collapse. The kingdom is generational, God's covenant was always described as "to you and your children." His plan includes the next.

Your fight will outlive you and the battles that you win in Christ will become the ground your children stand on. You set the standard, your legacy defines what "normal" faith looks like for those who follow.

Drills and Practice

1. Legacy Letter: Write a letter to your children, grandchildren, or spiritual sons. Tell them what you've learned, what battles you've fought, and why faith matters.
2. One-to-One Discipleship: Identify one younger man in your circle. Invite him to walk with you for the next month; share meals, pray together, let him see your faith up close.
3. Modeling Exercise: Ask yourself this, if my son imitated me in prayer, Bible study, speech, and self-control, what kind of man would he become? Adjust accordingly.
4. Physical Parallel: Do a weighted carry exercise (farmer's walk). As you walk, picture carrying faith forward for those behind you. The weight reminds you this isn't about you, it's about those who will receive the load after you.

Thoughts & Discussion Questions

1. What kind of legacy are you currently building, one of faith or one of self?
2. How did the men before you (fathers, mentors, pastors) shape your faith journey?
3. Who is watching you right now and learning from your example?
4. What practical step can you take this week to pass the torch of faith?

After Action Review and Mission Orders

1. What went right? Did you take intentional steps to disciple the next generation? Did you model Christ in front of those watching?
2. What went wrong? Did you neglect the responsibility, hoping "someone else" would train them?
3. How do we improve? Be intentional. Discipleship doesn't happen by accident. Your example must be deliberate and consistent.
4. Mission Orders: This week, do one deliberate act of legacy-building. Share a story of God's faithfulness with a younger believer. Pray over your children by name. Take a young man out for coffee and speak life into him.

Remember: Your mission is not just to fight your own battles but to ensure the next generation is armed, equipped, and ready to fight theirs.

Chapter 22: Live Faith-Fueled and Battle-Ready

Picture this, the air is thick with smoke, the ground shakes beneath your boots, and the taste of iron and grit coats your tongue. The campaign is nearly over, but the war isn't finished...not yet. The warriors are assembled, scarred and battered, their armor dented and bloodied. The Commander steps forward, not to congratulate them for surviving this far, but to prepare them for the final charge.

This is exactly where we currently stand...Right here...Right now.

You've trained. You've drilled. You've been equipped with every weapon and every piece of armor. We've walked through the lessons of identity, discipline, brotherhood, perseverance, and legacy. You've been sharpened for this moment. But preparation is meaningless if you don't step up and fight the battle in front of you.

Because make no mistake, the enemy will not go quietly. He wants your marriage. He wants your mind. He wants your family, your faith, your calling, and your future. He wants to wear you down until you believe you're too tired to swing your sword one more time. And here's the brutal truth, some men will fall. Some warriors will surrender. Some will lower their shields and compromise because the cost feels too high. But that cannot be you.

Let me share one more story with you from May of 1945. During the Battle of Okinawa, 26-year-old U.S. Army medic Desmond Doss climbed the steep face of Maeda Escarpment, famously known as Hacksaw Ridge while his unit was under relentless Japanese fire. As shells exploded and bullets screamed past, the battlefield became a slaughterhouse. Men fell by the dozens. Blood stained the rock beneath their boots.

When the order to retreat came, Doss refused to leave. While others scrambled for safety, he stayed behind on that hellish ridge, surrounded by enemy soldiers, armed with nothing but his faith and his determination.

All night long, as machine gun fire ripped through the darkness, Doss dragged the wounded, one after another, to the edge of the cliff and lowered them to safety using a rope and his bare hands. Seventy-five men. One night. One unarmed medic who refused to quit.

Later, when asked how he did it, Doss said he whispered the same prayer every time, "Lord, help me get one more." That's faith-fueled grit. That's battle-ready resolve. That's what it means to refuse surrender when the odds are stacked against you.

Friend, you are standing on your own Hacksaw Ridge right now. It may not look like a battlefield, but don't be fooled, the stakes are eternal. Every decision you make, every temptation you resist, every prayer you pray...it all matters. The question is: will you stand when others run?

Paul's trumpet still echoes from 2 Timothy 4:7–8, *"I have fought the good fight, I have finished the race, I have kept the faith. Henceforth there is laid up for me the crown of righteousness, which the Lord, the righteous Judge, will award to me on that Day—and not only to me but also to all who have loved His appearing."*

This isn't poetic flair, it's not a motivational poster quote, it is a battlefield declaration. Paul bled for this faith. He endured prison cells, shipwrecks, beatings, betrayal, hunger, cold, and rejection, but he finished. He never laid down his sword. And now, standing here at the edge of your own fight, the question comes to you:

Will you?
Will you step forward when others step back?
Will you choose faith when fear calls louder?
Will you endure when quitting looks easier?

Because you weren't called to survive this war. You were called to win it. You were called to live faith-fueled and battle-ready.

Every chapter of this book has been a weapon issued, a piece of armor strapped, or a battle strategy unfolded:

- The General's Orders reminded you that your life is not your own, you march under the command of Christ (2 Timothy 2:3–4).
- The Armor of God taught you that you cannot fight unprotected. Without truth, righteousness, readiness, faith, salvation, and the Word, you are naked on the battlefield (Ephesians 6:10–18).
- Prayer trained you to call in divine artillery, summoning heaven's power into earth's battles (Philippians 4:6–7).
- Brotherhood showed you that isolation is defeat, but unity is strength (Ecclesiastes 4:9–12).
- Discipline reminded you that no warrior wins without training (1 Corinthians 9:25–27).
- Resolve declared that suffering will come, but perseverance refines you into a weapon that cannot be broken (Romans 5:3–5).
- Legacy charged you to hand off the torch, to ensure the fight continues through the next generation (Psalm 78:4).

All of these converge here. This is the rally point. The charge is before us.

The stakes are not theoretical. Souls are at risk. Families hang in the balance. Your wife, your children, your brothers, your sisters, your community, they are either strengthened by your stand or weakened by your silence.

The enemy knows time is short. Revelation 12:12 warns us: *"But woe to you, O earth and sea, for the devil has come down to you in great wrath, because he knows that his time is short!"*

That means you cannot afford passivity. The lukewarm man is vomited out (Revelation 3:16). The idle man is overrun. The distracted man is ambushed. Only the faith-fueled, battle-ready warrior will stand firm.

So here are your final standing orders:

1. Take up your armor daily. Don't leave the house without truth fastened around your waist and righteousness guarding your heart. Every day is war. (Ephesians 6:13)
2. Lead your family as a commander, not a deserter. Your wife and children need to see Christ in you...not a perfect man, but a faithful one. (Ephesians 5:25, Joshua 24:15)
3. Stay battle-linked to your brothers. If you drift from accountability, you drift into danger. Pick up the phone. Show up. Lock shields. (Hebrews 10:24–25)
4. Train relentlessly. Read the Word like it's your field manual. Pray like your life depends on it, because it does. Fast, memorize Scripture, practice obedience until it is instinct. (2 Timothy 3:16–17, 1 Thessalonians 5:17)
5. Endure suffering with resolve. When pain comes, don't cry retreat. Remember, scars are medals in heaven's economy. (James 1:2–4, Romans 8:18)
6. Pass the torch. Find younger men to pour into. Don't let the chain of faith break with you. Be a mentor, a discipler, a spiritual father. (2 Timothy 2:2, Psalm 145:4)

Friend, I know you're tired. The battles you face whether it be temptation, discouragement, failure, or spiritual warfare,they wear on a man's soul. But hear me clearly: you are not alone, and you are not defeated.

The Commander Himself has gone before you. Christ bore the cross, conquered the grave, and now intercedes for you at the right hand of the Father (Romans 8:34). The Holy Spirit dwells within you, strengthening you when your own strength runs out (2 Corinthians 12:9–10). And the victory is already secured. Revelation 19 paints the picture: the King of Kings returns, riding on a white horse, and the war ends with His triumph.

You're not fighting FOR victory, you're fighting FROM victory.

So as this book closes, let me leave you with this Warrior's Benediction:

- Stand. Even when the world shakes, stand. (Ephesians 6:13)
- Fight. Not in your strength, but in His. (Zechariah 4:6)
- Endure. For the crown of life awaits. (James 1:12)
- Lead. For others are watching. (1 Peter 5:3)
- Finish. Don't stop halfway. Don't quit in the middle. Finish the race. (2 Timothy 4:7)

"Be watchful, stand firm in the faith, act like men, be strong. Let all that you do be done in love." (1 Corinthians 16:13–14)

The trumpet is sounding...The King is coming...The mission is urgent...The time is now.

Go forth and live faith-fueled and battle-ready!

✗ Warrior's Creed ✗
Faith-Fueled & Battle-Ready
I am a warrior of Christ.

I fight under the command of the King of Kings, not for my own glory, but for His. (2 Timothy 2:3–4)

I will put on the full armor of God every day—truth, righteousness, readiness, faith, salvation, and the Word. I will not march into battle unprepared. (Ephesians 6:10–18)

I will train my heart, mind, and body through discipline, prayer, and obedience, knowing that strength comes only from Him. (1 Corinthians 9:25–27)

I will not fight alone. I will lock shields with my brothers, stand in the gap for my family, and refuse isolation. (Ecclesiastes 4:9–12, Hebrews 10:24–25)

I will endure suffering with resolve, seeing trials as training that forges my character and proves my faith. (Romans 5:3–5, James 1:12)

I will lead with love and courage—serving my wife, my children, my church, and my community as Christ served me. (Ephesians 5:25, Joshua 24:15)

I will live with legacy in mind, passing the torch to the next generation, teaching them to fight the good fight. (Psalm 78:4, 2 Timothy 2:2)

I will not quit. I will not retreat. I will stand firm until the end, knowing that victory is already won through Christ. (2 Timothy 4:7, Romans 8:37)

This is my creed.

This is my call.

This is my fight.

By God's strength, I will live faith-fueled and battle-ready until the trumpet sounds and the King returns. (1 Corinthians 16:13–14, Revelation 19:11–16)

Author's Message

If you've made it to this point, I want you to know something first and foremost: I'm honored you trusted me with your story, even if you never put it into words. Pages like these are not easy to walk through. They stir memories. They expose wounds. They force us to slow down and face things we would rather outrun. The fact that you stayed means something. It tells me you're still fighting, even on days it doesn't feel like it.

My hope for you is simple, but it is not small. I pray that somewhere in these pages, you realized you are not weak for struggling, broken beyond repair, or alone in this battle. Trauma may be part of your story, but it does not get the final word. God does.

I also want you to know this: healing is not meant to be a solo mission. Isolation is one of the enemy's most effective weapons, but it was never God's design for His people. We were created for community, for brotherhood, for walking side by side when the road gets heavy.

That belief is at the heart of Warriors For His Glory.

Warriors For His Glory exists to come alongside people exactly where they are, not where they think they should be. We walk with veterans, first responders, and everyday men and women who are carrying invisible wounds and are tired of pretending they're fine. Through discipleship, PTSD recovery groups, faith-based mental health support, brotherhood communities, and practical training, we help people rediscover strength, purpose, and hope rooted in Christ.

If this book stirred something in you, if you felt seen, challenged, or encouraged, I want you to know you don't have to stop here. We would be honored to walk with you. Not to fix you, but to fight alongside you.

But whether you ever connect with us or not, hear this clearly and hold onto it tightly:

- God sees you.
- God knows your pain.
- God is not disappointed in you.
- God is not distant from you.

His love for you is not based on how well you perform, how strong you appear, or how quickly you heal. It is anchored in who He is. The same God who stepped into human suffering through Jesus Christ steps into your suffering now. He does not abandon His wounded; He restores them.

You are loved more deeply than you can comprehend. You are not forgotten. And the fight you are in is not meaningless.

Keep going.

Stay in the fight.

And never forget—God is with you, and He is for you.

Todd Woodfill